DALE WALKER'S
FOOL'S PARADISE

"My students from this region in Arabia always claimed
that *their* women were different, nothing like the hapless
creatures you see in the cities, garments fluttering in the
hot wind, all in black from head to toe like animated coal
sacks. Their women in that remote corner of Arabia did
not wear veils. Many of these villagers did not observe
Muslim practices. They had a custom of providing the guest,
the sojourning stranger, with one of their widows for three
nights.

It was obvious I had touched two raw nerves: women and
religion."

FOOL'S PARADISE

VINTAGE DEPARTURES

FOOL'S PARADISE

❖

DALE WALKER

VINTAGE BOOKS

A DIVISION OF RANDOM HOUSE NEW YORK

A VINTAGE DEPARTURES ORIGINAL, APRIL 1988
FIRST EDITION

Library of Congress Cataloging-in-Publication Data

Walker, Dale.
Fool's paradise.
(Vintage departures)
1. Saudi Arabia—Description and travel. 2. Walker,
Dale—Journeys—Saudi Arabia. I. Title.
DS208.W35   1988   915.3'80453   87-45975
ISBN 0-394-75818-8 (pbk.)

Grateful acknowledgment is made to the following for permission to reprint previously published material:

Henry Holt and Company, Inc.: excerpt from *The House of Saud: The Rise and Rule of the Most Powerful Dynasty in the Arab World* by David Holden and Richard Johns. Copyright © 1981 by Richard Johns and the Estate of David Holden. Reprinted by permission of Henry Holt and Company, Inc.

Alfred A. Knopf, Inc.: excerpt from *Looking for Dilmun* by Geoffrey Bibby. Copyright © 1969 by Geoffrey Bibby. Reprinted by permission of Alfred A. Knopf, Inc.

Viking Penguin, Inc.: excerpt from *Arabian Sands* by Wilfred Thesiger. Copyright © 1959, renewed © 1983 by Wilfred Thesiger. Rights outside the U.S. administered by Curtis Brown, Ltd. All rights reserved. Reprinted by permission of Viking Penguin, Inc. and Curtis Brown, Ltd.

BOOK DESIGN BY GUENET ABRAHAM

Manufactured in the United States of America

10 9 8 7 6 5 4 3 2 1

WITH THANKS TO JOHNNY, ISAAC, AND SARAH

FOOL'S PARADISE

F O R E W O R D

--- ❖ ---

When I got back to the States after my fourth contract in Arabia, it was with the intention of settling down and making up, if it wasn't too late, for all the work not done, and all the time frittered away in my heedless, bohemian years. I wanted to write, to call my bluff at last. Poverty, a constant nagging distraction, like a stupid fly in the room which keeps landing on your nose when you're trying to take a nap, was no longer an issue. Indeed, I had gone to work in Arabia once it became clear to me that I would have no peace until I got up and killed that damned fly rather than ignoring it in the lazy hope that it would go away. To make sure it was dead and stayed dead (I had only wounded it on my first contract), I had gone back four different times. On that fourth whirl on the petro-go-round I was so miserable that all I could think of was getting out. It wasn't the Saudis; I liked them well enough. It was the job and the *country*. After years of it, I had reached my limit and couldn't stand any more. A year's break in the States no longer worked its restorative magic. Like DDT in the liver, it was cumulative. I couldn't purge myself of it. I stored it, so I had to be careful about ingesting more. For every year I spent there swatting at the fly, though, I was haunted by the fear that a year's living was being deferred or lost. The gnawing bitterness of that fear—of *real* time slipping away (as opposed to what? Arabian, or unreal time?)—was poisoning me.

Every time I left, it was with the fierce joy of an escaped prisoner. As soon as my wife and I were airborne, or under way from the dock (once, to savor our escape slowly, we had taken a hajj-ship going back empty up the Red Sea from Jidda to Israeli-devastated Suez to pick up more pilgrims), there was no looking back. With our bank account stuffed with petrodollars, our senses reassuringly surrounded by the sights and smells of civilization (mostly the well-being that comes from cleanliness), we lifted our glasses "to life," as if what we were getting away from was not life but a kind of death, or limbo. Not that I didn't feel a kind of quirky pride at having been one of the "chosen." How many Americans, after all, had lived so long in the country? I had learned a lot about the people and their ways, but it was a kind of exotic knowledge, useless except as a curious ornament on the mantelpiece of conversation, like one of those souvenir shrunken heads a soldier in the Second World War would bring back from New Guinea. Moreover, it was an experience you couldn't readily share. That decade took a big chunk out of my life, but if I managed to get past this point at a party . . .

"Really? Arabia? Bring back any oil with you?"

" 'fraid not."

"Connected with the oil business?"

"No, 's teacher." (I had been through it so many times I had begun to mumble my answers.)

"Oh, yeah? What'd you teach?"

"English. English as a second language. I mean I taught young Saudi adults English."

"I'll be damned. Hey, those Israelis are really something, aren't they? . . ." If I managed to get past this point, and made a real attempt to fill in the gaps of my interlocutor's ignorance, I'd soon see his eyes glaze over with boredom.

So we ex-expatriates would find ourselves, once we got back to the States, more or less out of it. We had missed so much. We had gotten our America through overseas copies of *Time* and *Newsweek* (with the nudity Magic-Markered out, but not the Vietnam atrocities and Mafia slayings), so that as time went on we tended to see the U.S. as just another piece of the global puzzle, and to lose track of its local concerns. In other words, we were becoming colonialists, holding up for the natives and ourselves an exemplary Mother Country that was more mythic than real. But many of us chose not to live in that country anymore, especially those colleagues of mine who came to Arabia as young men and stayed. In their cases, Arabia had been the turf of their formative years; most of their best memories were associated with the expatriate life there. This was not my case. My going to

Arabia, in my thirties after the birth of my first child, was an acknowledgment that the free-and-easy days were over. It was time to corner that pesky fly and kill it, time *now* to interrupt my life so that I could get on with it later. Such was the attitude that sustained me: putting in time in order to buy time later.

That's what I told myself. Actually, I was becoming an old hand in Arabia without realizing it, although I should have: telling newcomers how it was in the "old" days should have alerted me to my true condition. Even during my detoxifying interregnums in the States, my network of Saudi and Saudi-connected American friends resembled the Saud family tree. If I needed any other warning that it was time to get out of Arabia, it came one evening on an Amtrak club car between Chicago and New York when, depressed by the conversations all around me in which I took no interest and had little comprehension, my heart gladdened at the miraculous sight of a pair of Saudi sandals on some guy's feet in the next aisle, as if I had been suffering from homesickness and seen something familiar! In a minute we discovered we had some mutual friends, and surrounded by our own incomprehensible countrymen, we clung to each other, a pair of homesick foreigners.

The fly was dead, or at least so thoroughly swatted as not to be a bumbling, buzzing threat to those sessions of sweet silent thought when emotion is recollected in tranquillity. My real work was cut out for me, and that was an enviable situation for which I was deeply grateful; I'd never get through it all. Yet I was restless. Newly divorced, I was learning that adapting to single life took time. I was discovering that divorce no more made a clean break in a human entanglement than sleep stopped the brain. Similarly, Arabia, while I had divorced it, wished it Godspeed and an affectionate farewell . . .

So I made arrangements to go back one more time, not heavy-hearted with a work-sentence hanging over me, but as a traveler in this ancient and difficult land.

PART ONE

ÄRABIA
TEHAMA

The haps that befell me are narrated in these volumes: wherein I have set down, that which I saw with my eyes, and heard with my ears and thought in my heart; neither more or less.

—Charles M. Doughty, *Travels in Arabia Deserta*, 1888

Jidda;
Mahatat Al-Jinoob

Arrival. Nostalgia for the "old" Jidda. Taxi driver tries to convert me. Islam the true religion, etc. Kept awake at the hotel by arguing Yemenis and wild dogs. Provisioning on Shara Gabel. Homosexual encounter. Choosing the hardest way to travel. Nomadism disappearing. The taxi station. Spitting Sudanese. Taxi fills up. I am sized up. Arabia before Islam. The pre-Islamic woman—any trace left of her in Arabia Felix? Women and religion very touchy subjects.

eat and confusion of a Jidda dusk at the airport. Dirt from construction and demolition, ground fine by the mad traffic, hanging in the air like a fog. Gaudy neon lights blinking on all the big new buildings: SEIKO, TOYOTA, BINZAGR. The caldron of the Red Sea sits steaming just out of sight.

The Red Sea! What romantic associations it used to have for

me. In 1969, when Jidda still had a recognizable shape and there were only enough foreigners for us all to feel like colonialists at an awakening but still remote outpost, the best hotel was a rambling place called the Red Sea Palace. One evening one of my brothers, whom I had not seen in a couple of years, passed through, and I drove the ninety miles down the mountain from Taif, where I was working, to see him. Johnny had spent years in the Air Force and had a truly remarkable ability to find an old friend in whatever godforsaken hole he happened to land in. Beside an open window overlooking the placid sea, a ceiling fan turned noiselessly overhead as he dug into his suitcase and put on the table . . . a bottle of Scotch. Scotch! Which I hadn't tasted for months! We called for water and ice. The black *Sudanee* brought a pitcher of water and a few cubes of ice in a bowl. Of course we didn't drink the water, but risked hepatitis anyway by letting the whiskey and the night melt the ice as we sat sipping, perspiring gently, and catching up on the last two years of our lives. We must have called for ice half a dozen times that night, hiding the bottle, naturally, and eventually even bothering to pour some of the pitcher-water down the drain when the *Sudanee* looked doubtfully at us. At three in the morning the last of the whiskey was gone. Here at the stagnant edge of the Red Sea, with only a few lights reflecting in the water (one of them ours), I was content to feel that I was as far from civilization as any character in a Conrad novel. Before we undressed to go to bed (lie down on the covers in shorts under the fan), my brother grasped the empty bottle of Johnnie Walker by the neck and stepped out onto the narrow balcony. (One has to be as careful with an empty bottle as with a prohibited full one. Consequently, the desert near the cities is littered with them, their labels sun-scorched.) He lifted his arm, there was a splash, the Red Sea Palace slept.

"It'll float right up to the edge of the restaurant downstairs," I said. Johnny opened his hand and showed me the cap. "No, it won't."

❖

That was thirteen years ago. Right now the middle-aged taxi driver wanted fifty riyals, or fourteen dollars, to drive me the three kilometers from the airport to the Red Sea Palace (now tacky and declassé, but I was staying there for nostalgic reasons). I bargained energetically, filling the air with comic abuse, and so startled him by my seeming fluency (I had mastered this kind of conversation) that I got him down to thirty. I put my suitcase in the backseat and got in front with him.

"Jidda's grown," I observed.

"Al-*lah* [meaning, God, *has* it]."

"When I saw it ten years ago it was a small town." (This for the sake of conversation. I had seen it much more recently than that.)

"What are you?"

"American."

"Al-lah. You Muslim?"

"No."

"*Ente quais,*" he said [literally "you good," but with the meaning that I'm a good man]. "You should become Muslim."

It is common for a Saudi to want to share the delights of Paradise with a well-meaning *hawaja* (outlander) who tries to speak his language and know his ways. It seems unnatural to him that one so enlightened in so many ways should remain obtuse in this one. The rare conversion of the odd Christian is written up in all the papers, and it's because deep in his heart the Muslim is insecure in his religion. That was clear right from the start, when Mohammed spent half his time defending his new religion against the ridicule of the Jews and Christians. So the conversion of a member of a "rival" religion reassures him, the same way the jingoistic American is reassured when a defector from a "rival" system sings capitalism's praises and proclaims that America is still the greatest.

If I became a Muslim, he pointed out to me as we careened wildly along with the honking traffic (he was doing his share of careening and honking) through the humid, dust-stirred evening, I could claim a job, a home, a car, a wife, and permanent residence. "Al-*lah*," I said under my breath, touching my passport. But just for the sake of argument I said, "I already have a wife."

"*Malesh* [Never mind], take another one. Saudi girl."

"Islam's too hard," I objected.

"*La, quais,*" he said. [No, good.]

"Good, yes, but *sa'ab* [difficult, hard]."

"What's hard?"

"Well, Ramadan. Can't drink water all day when it's so hot."

He pointed upward, sighed, and said, "Allah," as if to say, Well, you know how *he* is. "Do Americans pray?"

"Sure. Lots of them do."

"Are there Muslims in America?"

"There are some. They have their mosques where they pray."

"*Al-lah.*" Different pronunciations of that word can convey almost any meaning. In this instance it meant, *Isn't* that wonderful!

"Are there churches here for the Christians?"

"No Christians here. We are all Muslims."

"I mean for the *hawajas.*"

"No."

"Why? There are mosques in America for the Muslims."

"*Harram* [Forbidden]. Islam is the true religion."

14

"A friend of mine became a Muslim."

"*Alhamdulillah* [God be praised]. You can too. All you have to say is *la ilah ill' allah wa Mohammed rasul allah* [there is no God but God and Mohammed is his prophet]."

"But then you must pray five times a day."

"Yes, you must pray."

"See? It is difficult to be a Muslim."

"*Allah kareem* [God is generous, i.e., he will make it easy for you]."

"What if I didn't like being a Muslim and wanted to change back?"

He chopped at his neck with his fingers. "*Harram*," he said.

❖

At the Red Sea Palace, I tried to slip over the edge of sleep in prohibition Arabia without the nudge of alcohol. I never quite made it. Rather than lie under the drafty hum of the air conditioner, I shut it off and opened the windows: hot, but nothing like the shocking, unbearable heat and saunalike humidity that comes as summer deepens. The garrulous Yemeni watchman in the empty building across the way spent half the night "arguing" with a companion. Yemenis, like Beduins, converse in a kind of low shout that, to the uninitiated ear, has the hoarse ring of conflict. They probably were arguing. Yemenis sometimes murder each other here (and are beheaded for it) because they carry out of their mountain villages their ancient tribal feuds.

Finally they fell silent. Far off, the yapping of dogs. The Arabians despise the dog as unclean, holding it in about the same low esteem as we do the rat. Lower; if a devout Muslim so much as brushes against a dog, he has to ritually wash himself seven times and burn his clothes, or some such thing. By day the dogs are to be seen either asleep under cars, or else skulking about on the prowl for food, their washboard ribs and pinched bellies indicating constant hunger. There are so many of them, I am surprised they are not bolder. But a small boy, in the posture of stooping for a rock, sends them running, tails between legs. At night, however, especially in the wee hours of the morning, they come into their own, forming howling packs that I, for one, would go miles out of my way to avoid. In my insomnia I listen as one of these packs gets closer until they are right outside. Such a savage, furious din they make as they bark and snap (after a cat or whatever) that my hair bristles as I envision some poor early-rising Saudi getting torn to pieces.

I got up and looked at the place where the dogs were making their wild, furious music, expecting to see nothing but a blood-stained white dress, a pair of rubber flip-flops, perhaps a scrap of hair, but all was peaceful. On the open portico of the building across the rubble-littered sand reclined the two Yemenis on their pieces of foam, sleeping peacefully. Then surely a sheep or goat, foraging on cement sacks scattered throughout the ubiquitous rubble, has fallen victim to the pack of wolves? I look for fleece or hair drifting through the air; all I see in the windless May dawn is a swarm of mosquitoes, baffled by the screen, trying to get in at me. And now comes the first wailing, beautiful call to prayer ("God is most great! I testify that there is no God but Allah. I testify that Mohammed is God's Apostle. Come to prayer. Come to security. God is most great. Prayer is better than sleep!"), and a new day in timeless Arabia has dawned.

I'd rather sleep than pray anytime, but I decided to get up anyway and do some shopping. I had to outfit myself. What is a trip without a provisioning, an outfitting? If going on journeys is a deeply satisfying human need, which I think it is, the provisioning of one is even more so. Have you ever read a travel story without a long list, lovingly set down, of everything likely to be needed? I wish I could tell you that I had to go to the camel souk for this, the date souk for that, to the miller for the other, but I only had to pause on the Shara Gabel (Jidda's main souk-street) a moment, scratch my head, and think (with apologies to Doughty et al.): vitamin C. Yes, vitamin C to counter a cold I felt coming on.

Across the street between two money changers was a pharmacy. A dark, trim young man in a white *thobe* (long robe), his complexion marred by acne, stood behind the counter as if he'd been waiting for me. It was early. There was nobody else around.

"*Salaam alaykum.*"

"*Alaykum salaam,*" he answered slowly and meditatively, as if, while sounding the sonorous syllables, he was deciding whether he really wished me peace or not. I thought at first he could be a fanatic for whom the words "peace be with thee" are permissible only between Muslims. But he wasn't; he did wish me peace, and something else besides. When he put out his hand, he held on when I took it.

"*Keef haalek?*" he asked. [How are you?]

"*Alhamdulillah* [God be praised]."

"*Mabsoot?* [Well?]."

"*Mabsoot.*"

"*Alhamdulillah.*"

"*Alhamdulillah.*"

Among Arabs, this bandying of insincere formalities can go on all day. It was lucky that we were perfect strangers, because if we had been acquaintances, and had dragged the health of our relatives into it, we'd have grown old standing there. But when I'd had enough and started to withdraw my hand, he held on to it and scratched my palm with his fingernail. I *did* withdraw my hand then, I can tell you. Did I look like one of those worthless old Brits who've been hanging on here in the Magic Kingdom

forever? So much for my provisioning. I was so put out of coun-
tenance by this completely unexpected invitation to lewdness
that I walked out without getting the vitamin C. It was just as
well. The cold never materialized anyway.

❖

My way of paying tribute to my heroic predecessors who endured
hardship and danger while traveling in Arabia (for purposes very
different from my own) was to choose the hardest way I could
to go south. I had been invited to attend the wedding of a former
student off in some "lost village" (as Bob, my American friend
who had also been invited, called it) in Asir, the mountainous
southwest corner of the peninsula. Bob had assured me enthu-
siastically that we'd be the first "white men" to set foot there;
incentive enough, but I had still another purpose in mind, which
I'll get to shortly. I planned to go by GMC (or "Jimps," as they
call it), a ten-passenger carryall. I hate flying so high over the
earth that all her features become blurred and look alike, and
where, moreover, the only adventure likely to befall you will be
your last.

In case my resolve wavered, and I found myself looking en-
viously up at vapor trails while crawling along on the desert floor,
I had in my suitcase one of the greatest travel books ever written,
certainly the best book about Arabia ever written, Charles
Doughty's *Travels in Arabia Deserta*. Also on hand for quick in-
spiration was Wilfred Thesiger's *Arabian Sands*. These heroes
either walked or jolted along on camels (said to be more painful
than walking), surreptitiously making measurements and taking
notes while often faint with dysentery and fever. Compared to
such superhuman suffering, my gesture was an empty one. But
yet I had to do it—to rough it—and going by Jimps was as rough
as I could make it.

I could not have gone by camel if I'd wanted to. In 1960 St. John Philby (he and Wilfred Thesiger were the last of that great breed of Englishmen to explore the country) predicted that in thirty years Arabia would have no more camels. This in the *home* of the camel! At the time he was laughed at, but how right he was! In 1971, when two Americans, William Polk and William Mares, got permission from King Faisal to make perhaps the last trip *ever* by camel in Arabia from Riyadh to Amman across the great Nafud Desert, an experience described in their book *Passing Brave*, they not only had difficulty finding camels to make the trip, they barely found enough saddles, waterskins, and other accouterments in the junk souk to outfit their party. These "junk souks" are outdoor flea markets where foreigners have for years been picking up the fast-disappearing relics. Someday the only proof that nomadism existed in Arabia will be a conversation piece on some foreigner's mantel. I exaggerate, but not much. Almost too late, the government got a museum going in Riyadh, but I'd wager that my collection of Beduin "junk" in the basement of my house (collected over a decade of living in Arabia) is as complete as theirs. What was even more difficult for these American travelers to find were Beduins to accompany them. In one generation, the truck had wiped out a whole way of life. From the infidel West comes a single invention—the gasoline engine—and skills (and customs and mores) that helped them survive and adapt over thousands of years are lost. No, not lost: thrown away, abandoned, jettisoned, as one would toss aside, without regret, an inferior tool when a better one is at hand.

On the rubbly southern flank of the Jidda outsprawl, there is *mahatat al-jinoob,* or the south station, which is a sandy lot with several Jimps and about a dozen yellow Peugeot taxis parked on it. At the back, next to a cinder-block wall, is a tin-and-plywood shack. The morning sun, already hot enough to burn my face and scalp, had just risen. I took my suitcase off the backseat of the taxi and joined the driver where he was already in conversation with a nervous black youth of about twenty who approached as soon as we pulled up. The driver wants to be sure I'm in the right place before he leaves me. This is it, all right; the young black man explained that he'd soon be taking off for Muhayl. Muhayl? I'd never heard of Muhayl. Muhayl wasn't even on the Oxford map of the Kingdom of Saudi Arabia that I'd picked up. Not Muhayl, said I, *Abha* is where I want to go. He explained that Muhayl is the end of this line. From Muhayl you have to catch another taxi to Abha.

"How many passengers do you take?" I asked suspiciously.

"Eight," he said.

That was reassuring. The Jimps could easily hold nine. I was afraid they would try to pack in as many as possible, as they do in their little Toyota and Datsun taxis, five men and a driver. I wanted to rough it, yes, to travel like the new breed of urban Beduin (the lumpen worker), but I do not like my fellowmen enough to suffer being squeezed tight between two of them for ten hot hours. I wished I felt better. I was washed-out, jaded: up at four-thirty after a sleepless night due to jet lag and a drinkless evening. It seems that I had grown more dependent on alcohol than I realized.

The taxi drove off, leaving me with my cheap suitcase on the sand, the bag's imitation leather sides softened and sagging in the morning heat. I was adrift in this country. Good. Nothing I like better than finding myself in the midst of outlandish foreigners and barbaric yawp. I grabbed my suitcase and headed for the only shade, a wooden bench on the western side of that shack. Perched there was a coal-black *Sudanee* wearing a snow-white headrag.

"*Salaam aleykum.*"

"*Aleykum salaam.*"

The black driver took my suitcase and put it on the luggage rack atop the Jimps, then came back and recorded my passport number in a book—so they'd know who I was in case we had a head-on between here and Muhayl, I suppose. On the other side of the shed was a gas-burner and a pockmarked Yemeni who made tea. The driver ordered a glass for me but not for the *Sudanee*—who rectified this neglect by calling out in a good-natured huff that he wanted some too. He smiled. His teeth were so white in his black face that they hurt my eyes.

"You Turkish?"

"No. American."

"Ah . . . American. You know Muhammad Ali?"

"Yes."

"Muhammad Ali *quais* [good]."

"Yes, *quais.*"

"Muslim. *Quais.*"

"He's the greatest."

"What are you?"

"Teacher."

He opened his hands and showed me the calluses on his palms. "Me, *lavoro.*" He used the Italian word.

"Speak Italian?"

"Only some words. I work for Italian company here. I was in Rome once for a week." I was curious to know how a *lavoro* could afford Rome for a week, but I asked him only what he was doing there. Forces beyond his control. Was on a Libyan airplane that was diverted. Passengers were put up in a hotel for a week. "Roma *bene*," he said with a grin, meaning, of course, that it was nice to be able to sit in a café and order a beer, to see women and not walking black sacks (head-to-toe veils) on the streets.

I rolled myself a cigarette of White Ox black shag. "Want

21

one?" He didn't; in fact he had his own tobacco, a strong Iranian leaf that he put in his mouth like snuff, and then began spitting almost immediately into the sand at our feet. I went over to the Jimps and picked out my seat.

The driver was pacing nervously nearby, trying to look dignified and important but failing. So far he's carrying only two passports in his hand, my blue one and the Sudanese traveler's black one. "Where are the other passengers?" "They're coming, they're coming." I chose a window seat right behind the driver—safest place, I reckoned, in case of an accident—and put my plastic shopping bag there to reserve it. I drifted back to the shed, toward the only shade, but the structure was so low, and the sun already so high, that I could feel my scalp burning. I wished I had a headrag. The *Sudanee* was sitting with his bare feet under him, picking his toes. The tobacco must have been really strong, for it was generating prodigious amounts of saliva that he squirted almost continuously through his teeth, barely missing his flip-flops on the ground.

"You married?"

"Yes." (No need to mention that I was divorced.)

"Madame here?"

"No, in America."

"Ah. You children?"

"Yes, two. And you?"

"Also. Two children."

"Sudan *quais?*"

"*Quais,*" he said without enthusiasm.

"Any work there?"

"Work, but no money."

"Your madame here?" (I knew she wasn't.)

"No, Sudan. I go every three, four months to see her." He

opens his briefcase as if to show me her picture. I should have known better. Instead he shows me Sudanese coins.

"You Muslim?"

"No."

"Muslim *quais*. You should become Muslim." Here we go again. Do any other people in the world, I wonder, inquire of perfect strangers so anxiously about their religion?

"Why should I? I'm happy."

"Are there Muslims in America?"

"Yes, some. They have their own mosques."

His face lit up. "Al-*lah*." He spat contentedly onto the speckled sand.

Another couple of men showed up, a young Beduin with a dirty rag on his head and with a harelip—no, it's only a deep scar—and a tall, heavyset African. This other *Sudanee* was dressed in the loudest and most uncomfortable Western clothes possible: hot pink polyester trousers, too tight for him (I break out in a sweat just looking at them), and a shimmering green shirt with no cotton in it. In this climate, there isn't a better way of torturing somebody than to dress him in such clothes. To complete the misery, he was wearing shoes that had the poreless sheen of vinyl. While our driver was hoisting the suitcases of these two latest arrivals onto the overhead rack, I remarked, "We are only four. Anybody else coming?"

"They're coming, they're coming," he answered impatiently.

"How many? How long will we wait?"

"When we are eight we'll leave."

Over the next hour they drifted in, a bland young Pakistani who never spoke a word but grabbed a place right away on the fold-down seat in the very back; a comical old man chewing a *miswak* (toothstick, from a bush that grows near Mecca), carrying

23

a Sony radio, and wearing a dirty skirt that reached, Yemeni-style, only to mid-calf. His skinny, stiltlike legs were nearly black, and his feet, in worn-down Taiwan flip-flops, had deeply fissured heels. He had a sparse white beard like a Chinese sage, tiny simian eyes, and on his head was piled a rag that was once red and white. That wasn't all. Around his waist, like a sash, he wore an imitation leather money belt, and on his chest a T-shirt with the orange lettering of the University of Texas. His arrival on the scene was accompanied by a great deal of energetic bluster. Two other men drove up in a taxi and got out. A different breed, these: Egyptians. Each wore his *thobe* loose, flowing, like their native *galabia* (a robe similar in style but made with more cloth). In addition, they had their cuffless sleeves rolled up nearly to the elbow, which a Saudi never does. They wrestled cheap suitcases and cardboard boxes tied with blue plastic rope onto the luggage rack and took seats in the front, by the driver. One of them spotted me immediately and gave me a friendly, curious once-over: what the hell are you doing here, was the amused question in his eyes.

The old man was talking like a Beduin, in short, loud, staccato bursts. A joke was made about his age. Never mind that, he retorts, I get plenty of women. Oh, yeah? What do you do with them? The Egyptian, although he did not initiate the joking, was for some reason involved in the repartee. It went on for a full minute, with a thrust (laughter from the audience), a riposte (more laughter), almost like a comic routine or catechism they'd worked out, or like in those southern black churches where a kind of rhythmic chant is carried on between preacher and congregation. Finally, when there were twelve of us wedged thigh to thigh in the space for eight or nine, the driver collected a hundred riyals (twenty-eight dollars) from each of us and returned our passports to us at the same time. Then he got in next to the Egyptians, slammed the door, and started the untuned engine.

By this time I had been frankly sized up by all the men. While this process was under way I made it easier for them by feigning an interest in something going on out the window, so that they could satisfy their curiosity about me without my staring back. Obliging, wasn't I? While there were several nationalities present, I was the only real *foreigner*—a *kaffir*, nonbeliever. I stood out. I had as much business in their midst as that half-naked old man would on a Greyhound bus out in the middle of Iowa. I puzzled them. Nudging his fellow, one asked, What's that? (Not *who's* that, but *what's* that!) *Amreekee*, was the reply. *Wallah?* [Really?] They would have taken me for a Turk, a Jordanian, an Iraqi, anything but an American. Americans did not go by Jimps. Americans *flew*. Once they had looked their fill at me, however— a man more or less like themselves, only peculiar—they accepted the fact and forgot about me. Henceforth I was a fellow *rafeek* (traveling companion) who had cast my lot with theirs. At least, imbued as I was by accounts of the travels of my brave and adventurous predecessors in this desperate land, I romanticized my situation. The reality, as it always is, was somewhat different. These were not Beduins I was with, the Jimps was not a camel, the asphalt highway not a wind-effaced track, the gas stations we'd be pulling into were not dry wells. The only danger (a real one, though, when you consider their slam-bang way of driving) was the possibility of a head-on. Nor was my purpose in going south of any real importance, either. Did I mean to explore unknown country, draw maps, chart the crops and the rainfall? Was I sent here by the Royal Geographic Society, or by the blessings of a publisher? No, no, and no. It may sound silly, but

I had come all this distance to catch (in the fading light, as it were) the old Arabia before it disappeared forever.

To catch it before it disappeared forever, yes, but I also had the hope of catching sight of a certain kind of woman: a living fossil, so to speak, a rare, elusive, but perhaps not quite extinct creature: a Bigfoot, an Abominable Snowman, a Loch Ness monster, a relic of a time before Islam (which today has as little to do with Mohammed, its prophet, as Christianity has to do with Jesus) overtook a whole people and held them in thrall for fourteen hundred years.

Let me hasten to assure you that this quest is not an obsession of mine. If I don't come face-to-face with an actual living member of the species, I'd be more than satisfied to find a trace, a spoor, a sign that the old insouciant paganism has not died altogether. Here, if she still exists, is where she will be found. Opened to the world by highway only in 1978, Asir was the northernmost part of the ancient civilization known as Sabea, or Sheba, the Arabia Felix (the "happy Arabia") of the Romans. Scholarship has shown that in pre-Islamic times women had a status as high as it now is low; two thousand years ago these women had the kind of freedom that we think of today as modern. They were celebrated for their beauty and intelligence. They were often chosen to be judges. Some became queens. Under a matriarchal system (today Muslims refer shamefacedly to this period as the "Ahad Jahaliya," or Age of Ignorance) there were no permanent marriages but rather a good deal of promiscuity. A woman formed an alliance—a temporary monogamy—with a man of another tribe, but she stayed with her own people and kept the children. She could dissolve the alliance when she wished. She had independence and could contract business with anybody under her own name. How she has fallen!

But my students from this region (the Ghamdis, Ghahtanis,

Asiris, Zahranis, Jizanis) had always claimed that *their* women were different, nothing like the hapless creatures you see in the cities, garments fluttering in the hot wind, all in black from head to toe like animated coal sacks. According to these men, their women down in that remote green corner of otherwise wasteland Arabia did not wear veils. They worked side by side with men in the small plots and terraced hillsides of their fertile valleys. And I heard even more interesting revelations: some of these villagers did not pray or observe other Muslim practices; and they had a custom (this came out after I had described to them the famed hospitality of the Eskimo) of providing the guest, the sojourning stranger, with one of their widows for three nights!

This in Arabia! In adulteress-stoning Arabia! In Arabia, where women are so tabooed and bugabooed that it is bad form to ask a man how his wife is (or his sister, mother, daughter), lest you seem to be taking an unnatural interest in the womenfolk of his family. In Arabia, where, though for years you may be invited to a man's house, you will never see his wife, or his mother, or his sister, or his daughter. If, through some unavoidable mischance, a woman does speak to you, you will hear her disembodied voice coming, as at a séance, from behind a curtain. Sleep with a widow for three nights! In Arabia? Arabia, where women are not allowed to drive or hold jobs alongside male workers or attend classes taught by men. Arabia, where a brother or father would put to death a sister or daughter whose lack of chastity brought dishonor to the tribe. I first realized how sensitive this issue was when, talking to the other teachers about the class in which we had been discussing this pagan hospitality, we were overheard by Mansour, one of our student trainees, a tall, sullen Nejdi. Nejd is the area around Riyadh notorious for its intolerance, and in Mansour's black eyes fanaticism smoldered like spontaneous combustion in oil-soaked rags. He furiously demanded of me the name of the student who had been slandering Islam and Arabian women. Of course I kept his name to myself (the student was a Ghahtani, which is one of the largest tribes from the region, and a name mentioned in Genesis), but it was obvious that I had touched two very raw nerves: women and religion.

Breakdown;
The Gahhwa

Crammed together in the Jimps. Wind-blasted. The *hawaja* (me) outwits the selfish Beduin. Bypass Mecca. Religion and women. Breakdown. We wait for help. The agelong Beduin experience. The *gahhwa*, a desert hostel. Roughing it. TV in the middle of nowhere. Trucks that ply the desert highways. We are left stranded. Two Egyptians. Night under the stars.

Since Mecca is 45 miles east of Jidda, and Taif, a pleasantly situated town atop the "escarpment," 45 miles beyond that, I assumed we'd take the Christian bypass around Mecca to Taif, and then turn right, or south, to Abha on the newly completed mountain highway, a costly engineering feat (there are 117 bridges in the 350 miles from Taif to Abha) that opened the ancient camel route from Sheba to Jidda to the automobile.

The driver put on a cassette of Arab music, full blast, naturally, to compete with all the other noises, the main ones being the tires screaming on the burning asphalt and the hot wind tearing at the open windows. The scar-lipped Beduin youth wedged against me on my right was chain-smoking Kent cigarettes and dropping the ashes and butts unconcernedly at his feet. I groaned. Eight hours of *this*? Still, I reflected, there was no other place I'd rather be right now. This was a completely Arabian experience, wasn't it?—with the hot wind, the wild music, the crazy restlessness of the trip itself. Saudis are extremely rootless and restless, always traveling, always on the move as one completed road after another opens the country to them. They are like Americans used to be when the car and the highway were novelties and gas was cheap. Fortunately for my ears, the thick-haired Egyptian next to the driver was not so keen on having an authentic Saudi experience, at least where the music was concerned, for he shouted to him to lower the volume.

When we got onto the brand-new, six-lane superhighway to Mecca, the effects of our speed, combined with the *shamal* (north wind), made the open window next to me like a wind tunnel testing my head's aerodynamics. I was being blasted so fiercely that I couldn't open my eyes, and my lips were flapping uncontrollably as if a firehose were trained on them. My scalp, in its effort to keep my hair from being torn out by the roots, began to ache. And I was the only one affected! My young seatmate—joined all along my right side like a Siamese twin—was able to smoke his Kents in peace. Dammit, this was intolerable. I wanted to be a *rafeek*, yes, and share democratically the hazards of the road, but not a martyr. My smoking twin, however, obviously didn't give a hoot about the rules (or perhaps we hadn't read the same books). After I'd rolled the window three quarters of the way up, he promptly reached across me and, without a word, rolled it firmly right back down. Uh-oh. Trouble. Was I going to have to suffer this wind-assault all the way down to Muhayl, or was I going to have to have it out with this sullen character? I did recognize that he had a point; the wind was only really bothering me, and everybody else was squeezed in and hot farther back. But, on the other hand, why should *my* window be the one chosen to remain open, when the driver, muffled in his rag, had his window (the only other one on the windward side that opened) rolled nearly shut? Was it because I was a dumb foreigner, outnumbered and unable to look out for myself? A foreigner, a *hawaja* I was, yes, but I was not just any foreigner; I was a "Frank," as the Europeans (whether French, German, or English) used to be known to the Arabs. They even figured in one of those famous Arab sayings, something about God giving fingers to the Chinese, tongues to the Arabs, and brains to the Franks. To show that my tribe's ability to use our reputed gray matter had not diminished with time, I reached into my shopping bag beneath my feet and took out a large notebook, propped my elbow on the armrest, and held the notebook half a foot in front of my face at an angle that sluiced the wind nicely right onto Scarlip. I'm afraid I *gloated* as he tasted his own medicine. His headrag began to loosen in the gale. He couldn't smoke. His matches blew out. When he did manage to get one of his Kents lit, sparks flew off. I wouldn't have minded sitting like this for eight hours, but no more than two minutes went by before he reached across me again, still without a word, and rolled up the window. Shame on me for not showing Christian forgiveness, but I just couldn't resist a dig at him: "Had enough wind?" No answer. "Eh? Enough?" "Enough," he said, with as much grace as a rhinoceros in a trap.

Just before the old Christian bypass, at a point where the cars bound for Mecca were stopped by a striped pole across the road so the passengers could be verified as Muslims, we turned right onto a new two-lane highway. I had been in this general area many times before, but everything was so different now that I wouldn't have been able to identify it. This was America, this six-lane superhighway that we'd just left, America with its blue-and-white signs, not Arabia, not the Arabia of only two years ago. That's how fast things change here, not gradually but suddenly and completely, *bang,* as if these swarming foreign workers were stagehands changing the scenery between acts. Only recently, the road to Mecca was a wreck-strewn free-for-all, not a freeway. Now (since the shoot-out with Islamic diehards in Mecca's holy mosque in 1979) a car entering Mecca pulls into a kind of toll booth, where it is inspected for arms. But there used to be only a bored soldier—a sun-addled sleepwalker in a guard shack—who lifted the striped weighted pole above the old road when he was satisfied that there were no infidels trying to sneak into the holy city. At their peril! "How dire is the incertitude," said Doughty, "which hangs over the heads of any aliens that will adventure themselves in Mecca,—where, I have heard it from credible Moslems, that *nearly no Haj passes in which some unhappy persons are not put to death as intruded Christians.*" Christians (and Muslims who wanted to make better time to Taif) turned off at the guard shack onto another wreck-and-carcass-strewn road. It led them behind some low lunar hills that interposed between their profane eyes and the sacred city, and rejoined the main highway (with another soldier checking westbound travelers to Mecca) after the holy city was safely out of sight. If you are not Muslim they don't want you to even *see* their sanctum sanctorum, let alone visit it. You have to question whether people who live by such rules are in their right minds. This is not an idle or impertinent question. These are not boys playing clubhouse, a Tom Sawyer gang swearing a blood oath to kill those who learn or divulge the secrets of the brotherhood. A decade ago, when the world still seemed fragmented and compartmentalized, you'd dismiss such ridiculous behavior as unimportant, a mere comic or quaint or picturesque ripple in one of the world's weird backwaters. Now, with the growing awareness that the world is a giant interdependent organism, we can no longer afford to ignore what ails our brother, because, unfortunately, what ails him will surely ail us.

I don't know how it came about, but there used to be a kind of unwritten agreement that gentlemen did not find fault with each other's religions, no more than they would with each other's wives. I use this comparison deliberately. Religions are the totems of men, just as the myth of female chastity is man's creation and his totem as well. Look at King Arthur, riding off to war with his wife's name his battle cry, and her virtue his stay (she could be a whore, but she had to be his, nobody else's), although, as the invention of the chastity belt will testify, the poor cuckold knew deep in his heart that he couldn't control her any better than he could the fickle god to whom he prayed and sacrificed. Read the Old Testament: the Jews have always had a quirky relationship with their Yahweh that sounded more like a jilted lover's quarrel than a honeymoon. Religion is a man's thing, whether it is an Aztec priest tearing out a beating heart, a pack of savages whirling a bull-roarer on a string, or a man in a booth hearing whispered confessions, and it has as its common origin a fear of, and a desire to control, nature. And what is more "natural" than a woman's affections? A man does not fear his own lusts and longings, for he believes he is able to control them; but with woman it is a quite different thing. Because she is liable to come under the sway of the man she gives her heart to, she will adopt his language, his customs, and his gods, and she will be lost. This is what makes her sexuality so dangerous to men. The man's *property* is being stolen, whether it is done in a raid by a stronger tribe, or by a spoiler's sweet talk. How does a tribe humble its enemy? By capturing its emblem, its flag, its religious totem, its identity, and if it can carry away some of the wives and daughters as well, it makes the humiliation complete (and the revenge, of course, more certain).

Religion and women! We're talking about people who would kill the nonbeliever found in their holy places, about men who would kill any unauthorized male caught in the precincts of the *harram* (women's quarter). Is it any wonder that such a society would be so afraid of its women getting "independence," getting out of hand? Despite the almost daily reassurances by the *ulema* (religious elders) that Islam anticipates all the needs of mankind everywhere and for all time, the society is stale, stagnant, rigid, like a corpse around whose bier men gather. A religion is only an idea, or set of rules, one of many that governs men, and, as such, should be as open to inquiry, discussion, or ridicule as is the notion of free love, communism, or any other nostrum that is the common property of us all. One thing is sure: if a religion (or an idea) has to be handled with kid gloves, if you have to go around apologizing for it all day, there's something wrong with it; and if your wife has to be fitted for a chastity belt, there's something wrong with you. Religion and women!

So we made a right oblique on a new road just before the Christian bypass, and not a Christian among us, either. Half an hour down the road the driver fiddled with his tape deck, and the Jimps, as if it had been unwired, lost power, slowed, and rolled to a stop. What now? The driver turned the key to restart the engine, but nothing happened. In the sudden quiet, it was as if we'd become becalmed in a sort of highway Sargasso. To free ourselves from sweaty contact with each other, we all got out, all except the dour Pakistani, who had ensconced himself sideways, knees drawn up (he was wearing very white, very light-weight cotton pajamas) in the small seat at the very rear. The driver opened the hood. Several of us peered at the motor, to see if that would help. I leaned forward to jiggle the distributor cap, to see if it was loose or dislodged. As far as I knew, that was the only mishap that would affect the Jimps in such a way. But the driver waved me away brusquely, taking charge. We all looked hopefully at him. Conscious of his responsibility, he wound that all-purpose rag around his head with a new determination, hitched his *thobe* to his knees, and climbed onto the radiator, where he squatted, his feet so black and weatherbeaten that they seemed made of the same material as his frayed leather sandals. Brusquely he waved us aside again, announced impressively, "*Ana shugl* [I work]," and with that began to unscrew the butterfly nut holding the air filter onto the carburetor. "It isn't the carburetor," I said. "It's the electrical system. If it was the carburetor, it would have"—I didn't know how to say "sputtered" in Arabic, so I made a sputtering noise—"before it stopped."

He looked at me as at a pest and went on dismantling the carburetor. Then he climbed down and went to the back of the Jimps for his only tool: a screwdriver with a broken handle. Armed with that, he climbed back onto the radiator, hunkered there with simian balance, and levered off the metal clasps to expose the carburetor.

Some of the men walked a few score yards off the highway and squatted. There is a *hadeeth* (tradition) that Mohammed urinated squatting. It makes a lot of sense to do it that way if you wear a gown. It also makes sense if you live in a place where a strong desert wind always blows and you have to piss into it, which, to avoid facing the men at my back, I had to do to relieve myself (spraying my bare feet in the process). So hot was that ground-hugging wind that the drops felt cool. Yes, it made sense (and for all we know, the Prophet may have had trouble with his prostate, too), but the Muslim's obedience to religious tradition is such that if Mohammed had found it convenient to urinate lying on his side, I have no doubt he would have had emulators.

Twelve o'clock, the middle of May. I have no hat or rag, the Jimps casts no shadow, and my bald scalp feels as if someone is holding a blowtorch not far away. Secretly, of course, I am elated. Breakdown on the desert! What more could one ask for? I was probably the only one not annoyed by the delay because, for me, the getting there was as important as arriving. I had no commitments, schedule, timetable. Free as a bird, my only duty was to look about me and revel in the present.

When I got back to the Jimps, the young driver was mopping out the carburetor with a dirty rag. "It's not the carb," I tell him again, "it's the electricity. There's no power." To prove it, I asked Scarlip to turn on ("open" in Arabic) the lights while, to minimize the sun's competing glare, I cupped my hands around the headlight and put my eye close, looking for the pumpkin glow of electrical filament. Nothing. "There's no electricity." By now all the men were standing around the irresolute driver. I longed to take charge; it was the American in me, and, to tell the truth, coming from a technologically advanced civilization, I did feel responsible, especially since the Jimps was made in the States. But I decided to wait and see what Allah had in store for us. Finally, the overdressed Sudanese, who had the most to lose by a prolonged wait in the sun, suggested that the driver go back to Jidda and bring back a mechanic. But the driver, as if glad of a proposal, *any* proposal so long as he could demonstrate his leadership by rejecting it, said no, he would hitch a ride down the road to a *gahhwa* (*gahhwa* literally means "coffee," but on the desert it means gas, water, food, and lodging) and bring back help from there. Accordingly, he waved down a couple of rag-muffled Beduins daydreaming along in a Datsun pickup (when a driver is flagged down he always stops) and got in the cab with them while seven of the others crowded into the shallow bed, shifting the axis of gravity so perceptibly that I thought the little Datsun would tilt backward. But it moved forward with such undaunted speed that I was glad I was not in it.

There were now five of us left in the Jimps: the two Egyptians in the front seat, me alone on the seat behind them, the old man behind me on a seat to himself, and the Pakistani (way off in his other world) in the back. The windows on the right side of the Jimps were rolled up against the dune-building wind, which had increased until the surface of the desert was ablur with grains of sand on the march. Where there was a small bush or a tuft of dry grass the sand collected in the lee of it. Nobody said a word: our mouths were dry and our brains, benumbed by the Jimps-shaking wind, empty. I don't know why I stayed behind, why any of us did. It wasn't because of the suitcases on top. We didn't need to guard them. They were as safe there as if they'd been locked in a vault. There is *that* to be said for authoritarian rule. Before Abdul Aziz ibn Saud (the father of the present king, and the patriarch of the whole "royal family") unified this country by the sword, neither possessions nor lives were safe. In fact, many heads rolled, and many hands were lost, before the equation—crime equals punishment—was finally learned by everyone.

Behind me, the old man turned on his radio. Turned on his radio! Is this to him a Frankish miracle, or does he already take it for granted? Out of it comes a man's high voice, singing *suras* (verses) from the Koran. Actually, it isn't singing so much as a kind of high humming whine. It is really quite beautiful and has a long lineage and demography, stretching from the Talmudic cantors to the flamenco of the Andalusian Gypsies. Lulled by the voices (the old man whines under his breath along with the radio), drugged by jet-lag sleeplessness and the heat, I doze and wake, doze and wake, in the kind of drowsiness where one's head falls slowly and heavily to the chest, only to be jerked upright— by guilt, I suppose, although since I wasn't facing a dull lecturer or a stranger watching in distaste to see if I drooled, I had no reason to be guilty or embarrassed. The Egyptians in front were doing the same thing, and judging by the silent swaths in the ragged field of the old man's voice, I assumed he was too.

At two o'clock a Mercedes truck with high, gaily painted wooden sides (every flat panel decorated with scenes from Paradise: lakes, boats, clouds, trees) pulled over with diesel racket on the other side of the highway. Our scruffy driver jumped out of the cab carrying a liter-and-a-half plastic bottle of water: Sohat, from Lebanon, the label read, but its seal had been broken and the bottle not quite refilled with local water from the *gahhwa* ahead. Had it been filled at a ditch I still would have drunk it. I found myself staring at that bottle as the boy handed it to the Egyptian. Here I was, a middle-aged man, and I had only just learned what thirst means. Since a glass of tea at eight o'clock, I had taken in no other liquid. Now, six hours later, I was so dehydrated that for the first time in my life, water was a word and a *thing* that had real meaning. How quickly deprivation makes us selfish; I imagine that after another six dry hours, I'd have been ready to go to war for it. The Egyptian, whose moving Adam's apple seemed like a meter registering the water passing through it, tilted the bottle and drank. Four clicks on the meter. He passed it to his friend. Another four clicks. I was next. Half the water was gone as the Egyptian smiled shyly and handed the bottle to me. But what about the old man? What would the True

Beduin do in this situation? Is any consideration shown to age, or does one drink strictly according to one's proximity to the trough? I decided to find out, and passed the bottle directly to the old man who, much to my relief, indicated that I should drink first. (What if he had taken my action at face value and thought I didn't want it?) Mindful of the thirst behind me, I took two considerate swallows. The old man also drank sparingly and passed the bottle back to the Pakistani, who, because of our restraint, got a whole quarter bottle, which he guiltlessly polished off in five greedy gurgles.

Then our rattlebrained driver (why couldn't he have brought two or even *three* bottles of water?), with a pledge to bring back help from Jidda, climbed back into the cab of the Mercedes and roared off in a spew of black smoke and the dry grinding of gears. As the heat increased with the westering sun, causing the wind to blow harder, we soon lapsed back into lethargy. Imagine the Beduin Experience: thousands of years of afternoons like this one, sheltering behind their goat-hair tents, dozing, whiling away the time until the sun would set, the wind stop, the night come. The sand, some of its lighter grains blowing now at knee level, was drifting in streaks across the blacktop like driven snow.

The old man (the more I saw of him, the more he looked like a wizened monkey) lay propped comfortably on an elbow, fiddling with his radio. That was the only sound, that and the wind. Now over the radio comes the afternoon prayer call: God is most great! That loud assertion used to seem to me merely a meaningless insistence on the obvious, like saying "the greatest is great," or "there is nothing greener than green," until I realized that Allah, the god of patriarchy, had other deities to compete with. Before Islam triumphed about A.D. 700, taking the joy out of life by mandating prayer five times a day and prohibiting alcohol, Arabia was a much livelier place. Instead of one dour god, Allah the patriarch (Mohammed thought he was being enlightened by following the Jews and Christians in monotheism), there were three main female deities (Al-Lat, Al-Uzza, and Monat, representing the sun, Venus, and Fortune) and a slew of lesser ones, including local stones and trees. The Kaaba in Mecca (a big square building that the pilgrims circumambulate seven times) was a repository for their images, and the yearly pilgrimage to this shrine was a saturnalia, a trip worth looking forward to. A truce prevailed. A welcome breathing space for those contentious tribes was afforded in the precincts of the Kaaba. On the nearby plain of Ukaz the rowdy poets toasted Bacchus and held contests. There were no Miltons among them; their lines were polished at a campfire, not a desk. Doggerelists, they bragged about the brave men and beautiful women of their own tribe, and ridiculed everybody else.

Now the annual *hajj* (pilgrimage to Mecca) has degenerated into a month-long nightmare of clogged airports, traffic jams, and the threat of imported disease brought in by pilgrims. The pagan rituals have been emasculated, institutionalized, puritanized. The pilgrim puts on a towel (to show equality, so they say), runs between a couple of hills a few times, kills a sheep. As for pagan joy, you can find more of it at a convention of Baptist deacons. (In the old, pre-Islamic days, the pilgrims did better by disrobing altogether, which probably explains the Saudis' shamefaced reluctance to talk about their Age of Ignorance.)

At four o'clock some of the others who had been at the *gahhwa* come back with water, but once again it's not enough. Some of the returnees began loosening the plastic rope holding the luggage on the overhead rack. The tall overdressed Sudanese and another man took their suitcases and flagged down a young Saudi in a beat-up Datsun heading back toward Jidda. Another man, a short, dark Yemeni wearing a knee-length skirt and flip-flops, took his cardboard suitcase and got a ride in the direction we were going.

Forefeiting their fares, apparently, for the sake of movement. The rest of us sat and waited—for what? For our feckless driver and his miracle mechanic?

Finally, at five o'clock, two fifteen-year-old soldiers in a police car stopped. Talk. The policeman ordered the next pickup coming along to stop (a Toyota with three men in the cab and evidence that sheep had recently been in the back) by simply shouting at it through the loudspeaker, a noisy new toy on all the American-made police cars. This time, I am happy to jump in the back with the others. We took no heed of our left-behind suitcases, but I did carry my plastic shopping bag, as it contained my passport, address book, notebooks, and tobacco. After enduring ten minutes of wind-blast, we turned in to the *gahhwa* where the others of our party had been comfortable and well watered all day. I headed straight for the G.E. freezer, opened the lid, and reached for one of the stacked bottles of water, tearing off the plastic seal with my teeth and tilting it to my mouth while on my way to an empty *shai* (tea) bench. I sat down, propped up my feet, and drank at least a quart out of the bottle before I was satisfied. The label said "Najran water." Najran? That's a new one. Najran, which archeologists claim is very old and, like Mecca, was a place of pre-Islamic pilgrimage, is a town on the southeastern slopes of the Asir, near Yemen. A couple of years ago all the bottled water in the kingdom was imported from such certified wet places as Lebanon, or France, but Arabia for some reason decided to exploit its own meager resources. Now there are two local waters, both, curiously enough, from the two ancient places of pilgrimage, Mecca and Najran.

I called for tea from one of the Yemeni *gahhwa* "boys," who brings a battered quart pot and two little rinsed-out glasses on a wet aluminum tray and places it on the tea stand, from which I have removed my feet to avoid giving him offense. (It is an insult to deliberately offer an Arabian a view of the soles of your feet. Americans who like to swivel back in the office chair and prop their feet on the desk are warned against this practice before coming here.)

The *gahhwa* itself is a giant square slab of concrete, roofed on pillars but unwalled on two sides, with twenty or so benches scattered around on it. I heave a sigh of deep contentment. It is quite pleasant after the heat and glare of the day to drink sweet tea in the early evening, when the fierce winds of the afternoon have played out to a clean dry breeze. As Thesiger said after he had completed his lifelong ambition and crossed the Empty Quarter, his reward, after days of incredible and heroic suffering, was a drink of "pure, nearly tasteless water." (He meant not flavored with camel urine.) I rolled a cigarette. The *Sudanee* from this morning drifted over, his big white grin like the double six of dominoes. Having been sheltered in the *gahhwa* all day, he is still cool-looking and immaculate in his loose, snowy garments, whereas I am aware of being windblown, sand-blasted, and sun-scorched. I offer him tea and he accepts, drinking two little glasses before moving on. I'm sure he tolerates me because he thinks I know Muhammad Ali. Anyway, I am accepted now: ignored. No questions asked. A fellow-sufferer in a common mishap. I had not been selfish, I bore all with a shrug and a smile, I was all right. Actually, the people from this part of the world, though "provincial," are more worldly than the average rural American. The trade routes crisscrossing this ancient peninsula have been highways for outlandish peoples for a very long time; your average Arkansas hillbilly, on the other hand, or European dungheap peasant, only got a chance to see his own kind.

I hadn't given a thought all day to hunger, only thirst, but when food began arriving and I smelled it, I was all of a sudden very hungry. Don't get the idea that this primitive place was anything like a restaurant or café. There was no choice, no more of a menu than in a jail. There was only one thing to be had, fish and rice (you felt lucky to get anything out here), and if you wanted it you told one of the *gahhwa* boys who were constantly on the verge of falling asleep as they flip-flopped on their listless rounds. On a tin tray they brought me enough oily, cumin-flavored rice to feed a family, and on top of that rested half of a very large, porgy-type fish (the head and about four inches of body), plus a quartered raw red onion. No utensil of any kind. I grabbed a handful of rice with my right hand (the right hand controls what goes in you, the left is in charge of what goes out, and you never eat—or offer an Arab anything to eat—with your left hand), made a little ball of it, bent close, and shoved it in my mouth. Delicious. The fish was black on the outside but moist and white inside. Next to the *gahhwa* was a shed, or lean-to, where they cook. The fish was black because they fry it at great heat in oil that they never throw away, only replenish, so that it looks like something drained out of a 1929 Ford. The cooking vessel is a concave circle of iron, like a shallow wok but about two feet in diameter.

Standing next to the metal table, I ate all the fish, half the rice, and all the onion. The others chose to place their plates on the floor and sit close to them. All of us, however, wound up with very greasy right hands. Until you can wash it, it is not only useless, it is a serious liability. Doughty had the same problem. Here he is describing a "goat-grab":

The guests draw nigh, and reaching forth the right hands, in the name of Ullah, they begin to eat—rending their first morsels of the tail. . . . When they have done, the guests rise . . . ; in this wilderness-life, where is no superfluity of water, they wipe their greasy hands upon the tent-stuffs, or rub them upon their scabbards, the tent-poles or any saddle-tree by them.

Well, it wasn't that bad here; provisions for washing were just outside the front of the *gahhwa,* which is also where all the trash winds up. Soft-drink can tabs, cans, and plastic water bottles are simply thrown or kicked or swept off the six-inch-high slab of concrete, where they get scattered and trampled underfoot. Often the empty plastic water bottles get rolled by the wind out to the desert (those, and plastic bags, are Arabia's equivalent of our tumbleweed), whereas the aluminum cans get smashed flat into a kind of bright apron. A few yards out on the aluminum-paved sand, a fifty-gallon galvanized tank sits on cinder blocks. A brass tap at the bottom releases the sun-heated water, and a box of locally produced Tide detergent is at hand to cut the grease. One of the Egyptians, the shy, bushy-haired one, is there ahead of me. As he handed me the Tide he said, in an English-flavored tongue of his own invention, a phrase that sounded like "Good for wash hand." "Sure is," I agreed. A helpless smile from him, and a sound that approximated "Beg pardon?" "Yes, it is," I enunciated more clearly. He smiled. While I was at it I took my handkerchief, wet it under the tap, and damp-wiped the sand off my face, my head, neck, and out of my ears. Then I took off my shirt and scrubbed my armpits and chest. Nobody paid the slightest attention to me. Back at the bench, I draped the handkerchief over it to dry, and no sooner got settled with my notebook than an urge to defecate came over me.

One of the things I had forgotten to bring with me was toilet paper, something that is used only by foreigners; to Arabs its use, without water, is considered unclean. I knew better, of course, than to look around here for anything resembling a w.c., or toilet.

When I realized that I would have to go outdoors, just like a Beduin, a bear in the woods, or Mohammed or Jesus, I experienced a small rush of panic. I can't remember the last time I took down my pants in the open air, so to speak. I was a kid on a hunting trip, I think. And how to manage without paper?

I went out behind the *gahhwa* to look for something suitable, thinking what slaves we are to our conditioning, even the most traveled and cosmopolitan of us. Here I was, thrown into a tizzy just because I was forced to do something that I do anyway every blessed day of my life, but in an unfamiliar setting and manner. When I was in Taif in 1969 on my first teaching contract, living in the compound barracks, there was a Turk whose toilet training had taken place over a hole in the floor with a water tap at his left side. He was never able to adjust to sit-down toilets. Every morning he climbed on top of one, put his feet on the rim, and squatted. Then he would use the water in the bowl to splash himself (we could hear him plainly, his watery efforts sounding like a muskrat with a fighting fish), emerging from the booth to the basins (where other men would be shaving) to wash his wet left hand, a practice that the Americans found disgusting, and which did nothing to foster better international relations. In a Saudi bathroom there will always be that water tap (in the older houses, a wall cistern filled by a water carrier) and soap, usually Tide. If the house or apartment doesn't have a traditional squat toilet or a bidet, there will be a kind of poor man's bidet rigged to the toilet, a thin copper tube running from the shut-off valve, bent over the back rim of the toilet, then bent back up. When you reach down and turn the valve on, a tiny stream of water hits you right there.

Behind the *gahhwa* I came across an old cement sack (that the goats had missed) half-buried in the sand. It is true, by the way, that goats will eat anything; at least Saudi goats will. When I lived in Taif the herds of scavenging goats, wearing brassieres to keep their kids off the udders, kept the town remarkably clean. They disposed of everything but cans and bottles, which collected around the apartment houses. Every day I saw goats eating contentedly those thick dry paper cement bags. I often took a sack of garbage down, left it, and went back upstairs to watch from a window. Usually a cat, attracted by the smell of fish bones, reached the sack first, upsetting it and somewhat dispersing its contents. But when eight or ten bustling goats came along, the cat would retire to wash its face. Banana peels, coffee grounds, matches, cigarette butts and packages (aluminum foil and all), hard bread ends, eggshells, string, a pair of unmendable socks, a pencil, a worn typewriter ribbon, an old copy of *Time* magazine, boiled hops (I made my own beer), and the paper sack itself— gone. It was common, then, to open our door, four stories up, and meet a goat, face-to-face, on the landing. To get back to the business at hand: I tore off a piece of the cement sack, took it to the tank and softened it with water (the *gahhwa* boys notice but pay no particular attention), and then headed toward a nearby dune.

It was now twilight. The prayer call from the new cinder-block mosque nearby had sounded a few minutes before. There was nobody around. The dune was obviously a convenient spot, for behind it were ripe reminders in various stages of dessication. I took one final periscopic scan of the horizon to make sure I was alone, then undid my pants, held my breath, and disappeared behind the dune. Good heavens. In a country where most of the male population go outdoors all the time, you understand how practical their dress is, for it covers them like a tent. Their exposure is minimal.

A few seconds later (I didn't dawdle, I assure you) I stood up and rather breathlessly (as if I'd done something wrong and got away with it) pulled, buttoned, zipped, and adjusted my clothes, after which, with the edge of my flip-flop, I buried paper and all under a mound of sand. Judging by all the uncovered piles around, however, everybody else who went there was more dog than cat. Feeling good, even rather smug, as if I'd met a major challenge and overcome it (nothing like taking a dump outdoors occasionally, to remind ourselves that we are not to take ourselves too seriously), I went back to the *gahhwa*, washed my hands, and resumed my perch on the bench.

Twilight here on the *tehama*, a thirty-mile-wide heat-racked wasteland between the mountains and the Red Sea. The four *gahhwa* boys were eating now, seated on a fiber mat in front of the TV, eating the same fare (fish, rice, and raw onion) that we all had. They drank out of a common water bottle that they fill from the tank and keep cold in the freezer. The galvanized tank is kept filled by a Mercedes water truck that gets *its* water from a well, probably as far away as Taif. In all of Arabia, which is as big as the eastern part of the United States from the Mississippi onward, there is only one source of water, and that is the rain that falls, by far the most of it in the Hejaz and the Asir. Humid air from the Red Sea is precipitated as thundershowers in the mountains from Taif to Yemen, and it is this rainwater that eventually bubbles up in springs, wells, and oases at lower altitudes all across the peninsula, which slopes gradually from the western mountains to the Arabian Gulf.

As for me, I'm still drinking Najran bottled water, and I'm on my second big bottle. I keep it beside me on the *shai* bench and swig from it occasionally, just like the town drunk. I'm sorry now I drank that tank water earlier in the Jimps. The last thing I need is diarrhea, dysentery, amoebas, bugs, worms, cramps, or fever. Not that the underground water in Taif (if that is indeed where it came from) is not as pure as the artesian water of Najran, it's what may have happened to it from the well to the tap on the bottom of that tank that worried me. But listen to what poor Doughty had to drink: "The Beduins went to an hollow ground, to seek a little ponded rain, and there they filled the girby. That water was full of wiggling white vermin; and we drank—giving God thanks—through a lap of our kerchiefs."

The TV show is *Paco and the Lion*. I can't see the picture from where I sit, but I can all too plainly hear the narrator's Texas voice. TV! Out here in the middle of nowhere! I am now the only person left inside the *gahhwa*. It is very peaceful. I don't know where all the others have gone. I can see only the two Egyptians, the old man, and Scarlip; they had all moved onto benches outside as soon as the sun went down. Besides that Texas drawl, the only other thing to shatter the twilight peace is the occasional Mercedes truck that pulls off the highway with its loud diesel motor that has to be left idling for ten minutes to cool before the driver can turn it off. These trucks, which the drivers own and love as their fathers loved their camels, are covered all over with red, blue, and green running lights, and every panel is either painted in geometric designs or with scenes from Paradise ("gardens 'neath which rivers flow," promises the Koran to the believer after his lifetime's hell on this desert). Some even have loudspeakers mounted on the outside, to blare their jangling cassette music to the world. Truly, to see and hear one of these musical Christmas trees coming at you on the highway at night is to feel yourself in the presence of a weirdly lighted flying saucer from some civilization beyond the stars. These trucks are completely self-contained, carrying their own water, food, and bottled gas; and the driver, after cooking his lunch at the side of the road, will crawl under the high body for shade and doze on a straw mat through the afternoon heat.

At eight-thirty *Paco and the Lion* is interrupted for prayer, and on cue the *gahhwa* mosque sounds off through a loudspeaker mounted on its minaret. Don't they ever get tired of this praying? I wonder as I watch the *gahhwa* boys. Only one of them prays; the others busy themselves shaking the spilled grains of rice from their dinner onto the sand, rolling up their mats, and stacking more Pepsi cans in the freezer. One of them carries a plastic water pitcher off into the evening, to wash after relieving himself. The Egyptians, sticking together like brothers, head off in the direction of the mosque, and if the old man and Scarlip do not go there too, they disappear somewhere else. They have to. A Muslim does not just loll about indolently at prayer time, lest he be reminded of his duties. Muslims are ever watchful of each other. In Doughty's words, they fear the "reproach of irreligion." Islam today in Arabia is about where Christianity was in medieval Europe. In fact their year, 1400 (they count time from Mohammed's *hegira,* or flight, from Mecca to Medina to escape being killed by the Meccans), is a good indication of what century they are in as regards religious development. They are a long way from the Enlightenment. There is no Voltaire among them. During my first months here more than a decade ago, culture-shocked, appalled, depressed, and frightened as I was by the bleak, religion-dominated society, I had the distinct feeling that I had gone back in time a few hundred years into what narrow, fanatical, Christianity-blighted Europe must have been like, sealed as if hermetically and forever between its pagan past and its future glory.

After ten minutes of prayer-pattern silence from the TV, *Paco and the Lion* resumes. It is surprising that a dog (and not a Saluki, either, the hunting dog prized by the Beduin and the only dog tolerated by the Arabian) should be allowed on television when Miss Piggy, the Muppet, was banned because of *her* genus; perhaps Miss Piggy, pink and plump, might appear both edible *and* sexually desirable. Deciding to move outside with the others for the cooler night air, I no sooner select a bench with a firm rope bottom than our driver pulls up with another man in a Toyota pickup and proceeds to unload our bags on the sand. As he hands us each our refunds, he announces simply, "*Sayyara harbahn* [Car broken]," and drives off into the night.

It's always good to know where you stand. I was now completely on my own, without even that semblance of a lifeline, that unmaintained Jimps, to cling to. I was certainly not encumbered by baggage. Out of that pile dumped at our feet, I had the least, those Sisyphean Egyptians the most. As they push, pull, lug, and hump their possessions around their benches, one of them, the bushy-haired one, asks me if I'm Irani.

"Irani? No, American."

"Ah, American." This information seemed to clear everything up for them, as if they'd been trying to guess my nationality all day. But it also left them more puzzled than ever. Why wasn't I flying? they wanted to know, and liked me better, I felt, when I told them I wanted to see the country from the ground up. I was curious about them, too—who they were, why they were traveling south. They spoke no English. Well, one of them thought he did, and he was not ready to give up yet. It took him a full minute (you'd see him working it out in his mind) to get his something—perhaps it was Anglo-Saxon—out, but my response to it, and his reaction to my response, left us both . . . unsatisfied. It was pretty quickly established, however, that my Arabic, however faulty, was better than whatever he was trying so earnestly to speak, so we exchanged information in that tongue. Why was I going south? To see a friend in Khamis Mushayt. Ah. Where were they going? They mentioned some name. Village? Yes. Near what? Near Jizan. Did they work there? Yes. What did they do?

They taught. Oh! What? Well, the bushy-haired one, who spoke Old Norse with a Japanese accent, taught art! Art? Yes (he even said the word in English, "ahhrrt"). How long had he been teaching art? Only one year. But his friend had been carrying the torch of science down in that lost village for four years. Did they like the life? Well, not especially . . . no, not really . . . but it was a living. Art! Making a living teaching *art* down near the Yemen border! I felt so sorry for the poor guys, as de Tocqueville, traveling in frontier America a century and a half ago, would have instinctively had his gentlemanly sympathies aroused if he had run across a pair of fellow Europeans who, down on their luck, were heading out to, say, Pecos, Texas, to teach music, or ballet, or some other useless luxury of civilization, to the rustics.

One of the *gahhwa* boys began distributing foam-rubber mattresses, foam pillows with dirty cases, and blankets to us and to another couple of men who had stopped and were going to spend the night. Five riyals (a dollar and a half) for the rent of them. To make sure I didn't wake up thirsty and find the *gahhwa* boys asleep, I prudently bought another bottle of Najran water, filled my pipe again, and with my back to a vertical bar of white neon light on a pole behind me, I faced the neon-lit *gahhwa* and wrote up my notes.

It is quite an impressive oasis, a bright galaxy in the blackness, and if, to my refined taste, it is gaudy and garish, I can understand how, to a Saudi, the more emphatically the night is electrified, the better. It's the same with his electronic gadgets. Whereas we Westerners seek soft light, off-whites, and low decibels, the Saudi (and in fact the whole Third World) craves raw, night-defying neon, bright reds and purples to enliven his tanned landscape, and full-throated amplification to banish silence. This *gahhwa* has it all: light, color, noise. Although the TV is watched only desultorily now, it blares on until the station plays the national anthem (a martial piece that a Frenchman was commissioned to write) and goes off the air. But there is still a great deal of vocal energy until very late as the *gahhwa* boys, revived by the cool night, shout at each other as they sweep down and clean up (it all goes right out in front). On this, my second night without alcohol (a word, ironically, derived from the Arabic—*al-kuhul*—of better days), I do not feel at all inclined to sleep, but I spread my handkerchief over the dirty pillow, lie down anyway, and look up at the stars. Alas, a disappointment. Because of the competing light from the *gahhwa*, I can see them better from my own backyard.

One of the things you don't get in my backyard is a prayer call at 5:00 A.M. It is loudspeakered from the *gahhwa* mosque out to the astonished jerboa, little desert rodents whose bright-eyed cuteness doesn't save them from the pinch-bellied hunger of the Beduin. Allah! Amplification in the service of Islam. The ulema, religious elders who oppose innovation on the grounds that if Mohammed could live without it, so can we, only softened its opposition to the introduction of radio and TV after it was demonstrated that these snares of *shaytahn* (Satan) were also capable of broadcasting prayer over a wider area. A Muslim fundamentalist is not much more enlightened than a hardshell Baptist. They are both motivated by the same impulse: to make their neighbors as unhappy as they are themselves. Many of these wet blankets are, of course, pious humbugs and hypocrites. It is well known that opportunities for lecherous encounters with ecstatic females abound in the revival tents of the Bible Belt, and as an example of the kind of contradictions practiced by a hardshell

Muslim, I have the word of Keith (Abdullah) Garrison, a friend and fellow teacher who converted to Islam.

Keith was a sort of religion junkie, so his conversion, while it was a big deal to the Saudis (proof, as I have pointed out, of the noninferiority of their religion), was something of a joke to those of us who knew him, like seeing the town slut go across the valley, where she wasn't known, pass herself off as a virgin, and marry the preacher's son. Keith started as a Catholic, but he had been a Buddhist, Zen Buddhist, Hindu, Mormon, Holy Roller, you name it. He converted to Islam as easily and as mindlessly as a nice middle-class girl from Long Island joining the Moonies. At any rate, every convert to Islam is quickly surrounded by spiritual advisers, and Keith was no exception. Poor fellow, he believed more in Islam's spirit (compassion, mercy, forgiveness) than in its literal letter as promulgated by some of its uncompassionate, unmerciful, and unforgiving interpreters. In that stance he found himself in the minority. There were times when, in the heavy afternoon-nap time, he found it *not better* to pray than sleep, but he was seldom left alone. He was now a Muslim brother, with many keepers. And there were times when, about midway through a hot Ramadan day, he would have liked, with the help of a cup of coffee and a cigarette, to relax, to catch his breath, as it were, and take a *broader view* of Islam, but he always had someone close at hand to hold him to the straight and narrow. (In the month of Ramadan, which advances by eleven days each year because of their lunar calendar, no food, liquid, or smoke may pass a believer's lips from dawn to dusk. The purpose of this is to turn life on its ear, to look at it in a new way, break the degrading routine of everyday life by reversing night and day. In Ramadan, you are supposed to be especially generous to the unfortunate. The month culminates in gift-giving and visiting back and forth, rather like our Christmas.) But hadn't Keith been renamed *abd* (slave) *ullah* (God), the slave of God? Now, one of those advisers was his landlord who wouldn't allow tenants to smoke or own TV sets. Religious fanatics consider smoking intoxicating (Arabic uses the same verb for smoking and drinking), hence the sale of cigarettes was prohibited until a few years ago. TV, because it shows pictures of people (the "images" forbidden by Allah) is also anathema. So anathema, in fact, that King Faisal, brother of the present king, lost his life in a roundabout way over the issue of television.

The ulema, as I have said, first opposed it but then gave their consent. A band of diehards, however, ridiculing the ulema as a bunch of old men who secretly planned on nodding away their last years in front of a TV set, marched on the new station in Riyadh with the intention of destroying it, and were fired on by the National Guard. Killed that day was Khalid ibn Musa'id, one of King Faisal's nephews. Ten years later, in March 1975, Faisal ibn Musa'id, another nephew, brother of the slain one, shot his uncle in the face in his office, thus avenging his brother's blood and his own honor according to the ancient code of the desert. A Saudi does not kill an enemy and then try to beat the rap by reason of insanity or some such excuse. He would consider such an action effeminate and cowardly. On the contrary, he is proud of what he has done, and faces his own certain death by public execution bravely.

One of my students who had been there described to me Musa'id's execution in June 1975. With his long black hair (he had lived in the States and was something of a hippie) falling over the shoulders of his clean white *thobe*, Musa'id was led out before the crowd on a Friday just after the midday prayers and forced to his knees. It was his misfortune that his uncle was a beloved king, to many Saudis the real father of the country, and vengeful emotions were running high. My student said that the executioner (an ex-slave who has been rewarded for his years of faithful service and lives in a sumptuous villa in Jidda) had asked that Musa'id's hair be left uncut, and that the first thing he did was grab it and slice it off with his razor-sharp sword, because, as he taunted his victim, he "could not kill a woman, but now that he was a man, or half a man. . . ." He next began slicing at his shoulders: "Kill a king, will you?" he taunted, cutting across his back, the white *thobe* turning red. "Shoot him in the face, will you?" he went on, working himself into a fury, Musa'id flinching under the cutting but not crying out. Until, with the sharp, square-filling *chop* of steel striking bone, such as you hear from the butchers in the meat souk every day, it was over. The body was allowed to lie there all afternoon. The head was stuck on a nearby pole and left all night.

It is clear that religion is taken very seriously here, and this landlord, Jehan, warned Keith to get rid of his TV set *and* his gold ring, because of a *hadeeth* that relates that one day Mohammed threw the gold ring of a visiting rich man into the fire. So Jehan, pious Muslim, wears no gold (since it was a *man's* gold ring that Mohammed threw into the fire, gold is worn by women without guilt), but he drives a new Mercedes, has a telephone, and flies in airplanes.

It is pleasant, in the cool dawn, to drink the weak sweet tea just brewed by a *gahhwa* boy and to watch the sun rise over the mountains in the east. Now that the day has taken over, the neon is switched off, and the Magic Oasis of the night now sprawls as a sun-overwhelmed, desert-daunted, drab, oil-stained horror. Pleasant, I say, to sit here and realize that this Saudi Arabia— this sandy *gahhwa* with its delta of flattened Pepsi and Vimco cans—is in transition just like the American highway was in the thirties at the dawn of automobile travel. The transformation here, however, will not be gradual but overnight. Even now, modern, clean gas stations are going up near the cities. In a few years, traveling in Arabia will be as comfortable, as uneventful, and as plastic as on an American interstate, for such seems the will of the country.

❖

Foothills of the Asir

We hitch a ride. Beehive houses. Abdullah the guide. Leaving the sunstruck *tehama*. Stone houses and guard towers. Abdullah guards his tribal name. Egyptian mimics our black driver. Blacks in Arabia. Legend of the hospitable widow. Stop for tea. Arabian egalitarianism. Reckless drivers. Egyptians go on alone. Muhayl. The Semitic race. A walk around the souk. A crippled dog. An old horse. The *gahhwa*. The Land Cruiser. I share a seat with a huge Sudanese. The "short-cut" to Abha. Inches from disaster. The top of the escarpment. Stop for prayer. Another world.

here were now only three of us: the two Egyptians and myself. Sometime during the night the old man and Scarlip had vanished. As I drank my tea and called out *sabaa al hayr* (literally, "morning the light") to my two companions, I had no idea how I'd get to Muhayl. But I knew that I'd get there somehow, and was not troubled. Right now, though, first things first: tea and a smoke. Contrast my feeling of complacent safety with Doughty's dangerous insecurity: "I considered how desperate a thing it was, to be abandoned in the midst of the wilderness of Arabia, where we dread to meet with unknown mankind more than with wild beasts." We were a grubby, unshaven threesome in that morning light, especially the Egyptian whose thick hair, in contact with the foam *gahhwa* pillow all night, gives him the appearance of having slept in a tree. After I paid my two pocket-crumpled one-riyal bills to a *gahhwa* boy for a pot of tea, I went out behind the dune to piss. I freshened my face at the water tank with my wet handkerchief, then I carried my suitcase to the highway and stood beside it, with the sun, already hot enough to warm up yesterday's burn, in my face. The Egyptians do the same, positioning themselves about twenty yards away, a distance I know they chose delicately in case I needed room to maneuver on my own. They had left their bulky luggage out of sight down by the *shai* benches. I had an intuition they would include me in whatever arrangements they made, so I just stood there passively stranded, a fate-becalmed *hawaja* in Arabia Tehama.

Every pickup that the Egyptians flagged down stopped, but the three trucks that came along over a quarter-hour period either had excuses, after looking us over, for not taking us (three foreigners, after all, one of them standoffish) or were not going to Muhayl. The fourth vehicle, a brown, canvas-topped Toyota Land Cruiser driven by a clean-shaven young man, stopped, and after a *salaam aleykum* and a handshake, the driver, Abdullah, entered into a discussion with the Egyptians. After a minute the teacher of art took me aside: "We told him we'd pay him the regular hundred-riyal fare. Okay with you?" "Fine," I agreed. I offered the money to the driver then and there, but he waved it away as he pulled up to a gas pump. "Lucky for you I was running on empty," he explained, perhaps a little grudgingly, resenting our luck, "I had to stop here anyway."

On our way again in Abdullah's Land Cruiser, we barreled along at 120 clicks an hour over terrain as sorry as any the earth has to offer. You'd have to go to Mars to find worse. I was in the front seat next to the driver, my suitcase propped between us; the Egyptians, with all their luggage, were in the back. I had politely tried to take the most uncomfortable place for myself, but the Egyptians anticipated me and wouldn't hear of it.

"No, you go in front. You can see better there."

"I can see out the back window."

"Absolutely not. We will ride in back."

"It isn't fair for you to ride in back."

"We've seen the country before. You haven't." Finally the bushy-haired one said in his peculiar English, "Please. Take rest."

"Okay, but only for a while, then we'll change."

Abdullah and the Egyptians began discussing me. Although I could not follow all of the rapid exchange, it was obvious that they were praising me to Abdullah as a gentleman. Now Abdullah put some questions of his own to me: where I was going, why I wasn't flying, etc. I answered in the usual way, and after that he became quite friendly, assuming the role of guide, in fact. He did this by touching my arm, which lay atop my suitcase, then pointing at something. Actually this came later. For the first couple of hours there wasn't anything to point out, but as the malaligned, canvas-topped Land Cruiser vibrated and flapped southward with its gas pedal to the floor, the scenery got a trifle more interesting. It was still a long way from being a poster on a travel agency wall, but at Al-Lith, a village marked on my Oxford map (as I spread the map on my knees Abdullah looked at it as at a marvel), I saw for the first time those beehive-shaped houses peculiar to the *tehama* of southern Arabia. Abdullah did not point them out; apparently he saw nothing unusual or interesting in them. It is hard to know what a Saudi considers interesting or beautiful. Wilfred Thesiger, in *Arabian Sands*, observed, "But while they are very sensible of the beauty of their language, they are curiously blind to natural beauty. The colour of the sands, a sunset, the moon reflected in the sea: such things leave them unmoved." Three things that they all like are green grass, running water, and cloudy skies.

After Al-Lith there were several villages in a row—Hamdanah, Ad-Duqah, Al-Qunfidhah—each, only a few years ago, a long two-days' camel ride apart. But in Abdullah's Land Cruiser it was only thirty shimmying minutes, and in that high speck of aluminum, its underbelly frosty-white in the morning sun, whose hawk's shadow swept over us in the blink of an eye, less than one. The morning flight from Jidda to Abha. Businessmen (Beduins' sons) up there with briefcases, going to Asir to buy land, make deals, import and export, buy and sell. Unbelievable.

At Kidwat al-Awaj, marked as a "village" on my map, but only a crossroads *gahhwa* in reality (with a few of those thatched beehives floating in hallucinatory mirage on some forlorn dunes), we stopped for gas and refreshments. The word *village* connotes a picturesque, small but fixed settlement that has some reason for being, with surrounding land to be farmed, or a nearby sea to be fished. But when I say "village" in this part of oven Arabia, it is because English lacks a word to describe what I am seeing: a most dismal sprawl of brush houses scattered along several hundred yards of sand dunes. These beehive huts are built very like the Indian teepee: a dozen poles lashed together at the top and spread out to form a room of about ten or twelve feet in diameter. Between the vertical poles, other poles will be fixed horizontally, a couple of rows of them, and the interstices filled in with dry desert bushes, twigs, or thatches of sorghum stalks, which is cultivated in patches from here southward. They are little more than windbreaks, only slightly more permanent than the Beduin's goat-hair tent, but, because of this, a hundred times more unsightly. The Beduins moved on and did not pollute; these beehive "villages" look as though, on some night of mischief, a large supermarket were looted, its entire contents strewn around everywhere recklessly, and then smashed flat. At a small *dukkan* (store: imagine a very large packing crate, its walls filled with imported goods, open in front where the proprietor, picking at his plump brown toes, sits cross-legged on a flattened cardboard box on the littered sand), we each bought a plastic bottle of cold Najran water to swig on, got back into the Land Cruiser (the Egyptians again beating me to the back, urging me to "take rest"), and turned left, or east, toward the mountains, leaving the fierce heat of the *tehama* and the steamy Red Sea behind (and below) us.

We started climbing almost immediately and followed the road along a *wadi* (watercourse). We went through so many giant boulders and rocky outcroppings—the beginnings, or the broken-off pieces, of that range ahead of us—that our Land Cruiser was absurdly dwarfed, like an ant in a gravel pit.

"Good road," I commented appreciatively.

"Two years old," said Abdullah, touching my arm with a henna-dyed fingernail to get me to look ahead toward a narrow but open valley where several old stone houses sat decaying. (Many women dye their palms, heels, and toes, but Abdullah hennaed his fingernails and toenails.) The sight of those houses quickened my heart. Here was something entirely new in Arabia. Water stood here and there in pools, giving life to small green patches of cultivation alongside them, and watching over it all was a round stone tower. At some distance from the crumbling stone houses—joined together atop a rise, they looked like half-rotted molars in a gum—stood a new cinder-block "villa" surrounded by a head-high cinder-block wall painted a light green. Every new Arabian house has this unsightly barrier (most are not even painted), so jealous are they of their (read women's) privacy. Next to an iron gate cemented in the wall was parked a new Peugeot station wagon, but in this tiny oasis there were no other signs that anyone lived there. Once, obviously, judging by the crumbled-down stone houses, this bucolic spot supported an extended family that, in "this insecure Semitic world," as Doughty called it, had to guard itself against all the other neighboring extended families. When I asked Abdullah what was the purpose of that dark brown stone tower, which was about the height and color of a Manhattan brownstone and the girth of a factory smokestack, he took both hands off the wheel for a second, held an imaginary rifle, aimed, and said, "That's what they were for in the old days."

How old is "old"? Only a hundred years ago, when Doughty was traveling in Nejd, the towers were *used*:

As the sun came up we descended to a plain, and I saw the palms of a . . . Kasim village. . . . We found some of the village women busy abroad to cut fodder for their well-camels. Those hareem cried out, supposing we might be robbers, till we said *salaam!*—They were come forth in their old ragged smocks for dread of thieves . . . a few days ago some of their women had been stripped by Beduins a little without the village walls! Four miles further . . . upon a cliff by the Nefud side is a clay-built lighthouse-like watch-tower (. . . found in all the villages of Kasim). The watchman (who must be clearsighted) is paid by a common contribution.

"What *bilad* [tribal turf] are we coming into?" I asked Abdullah.
"Shahran."
"Are you a Shahrani?"
"*La* [No]," was all he answered. I didn't ask him then what *was* his tribal name, for I knew that he wouldn't want to tell me. While a man's tribal name used to be his only protection in a savage world where every man's hand was against all others, it could also be, among strangers, his death sentence, as Doughty wrote:

> It was not long before we saw a glimpsing of Beduin watchfires. We arrived so silently, the dogs had not barked. . . . When the Aarab perceived us, all voices were hushed: their cheerful fires, where a moment before we saw the people sitting, were suddenly quenched with sand. . . . Alighting in silence, we sat down a little aloof: none of us so much as whispered to his companion by name; for the open desert is full of old debts for blood.

The "old days" indeed. Just as a Saudi does not want to talk about the Age of Ignorance, that embarrassing pagan skeleton in his closet, so likewise he would rather steer the conversation away from the time just preceding our own, when Ibn Saud, a young *sheikh* (strong leader) out of Riyadh, conquered, pacified, and "unified" the tribes by fire and sword and gave his name to it all. The history of Arabia is little else but squalid tribal warfare. Occasionally, over this long lethargic span of history–forgotten time, several of the tribes, under a sheikh, would confederate to gang up on some other ones. But as soon as that leader was killed, the unstable alliance would come apart, like a game of pirates played by fickle boys. Back they would go to the desperate lethargy of their desert poverty. Once again it would be the timeless law of every tribe for itself. But this time, held together by the incredible luck of found wealth (the dream of every Arabian come true!), the peace that the Saud clan imposed on these "most miserable of mankind" (as Doughty called them), is likely to last.

The Arabs of Arabia have always been governed by force. People who mistakenly recommend a softening of the strict rule into something more "democratic" don't know this wild country. What is needed, in the opinion of many, is a couple of generations *more* of this firm (and time-honored) rule, this paternal despotism over a household of unruly children, as it were, to let those "old debts for blood" be forgotten.

Higher up into the wadi we came more frequently upon those crumbling houses and towers. The old houses of southern Arabia are entirely functional and beautiful, the people's only indigenous art form, and as long as I was there I never tired of seeing them. *Tired?* I should say I was charmed. The mere sight of one refreshed the eye as water cooled the throat, and made me feel good all over: light and cheerful and hopeful for the human race. I gave the people who built such graceful aeries the benefit of the doubt right away. The sheer amount of *work*—the millions of flat stones, hand-placed one on the other and chinked so carefully with smaller shards that mortar was unneeded, and the eye could discern no imperfections in the plumb-straight lines—gladdened the oppressed heart in shiftless, make-do, slapdash, and prefab modern Arabia. It was like coming into a foreign country, an old and civilized foreign country. The air was better too. Near the Red Sea the humidity is so thick that sky, horizon, and houses blur together in a kind of indistinct haze, like objects and shapes

in a Turkish bath. But these old houses stood etched in a pure, hard light.

Our spirits rose in this lighter air and we began chatting. The Egyptians were telling Abdullah about our adventures on the road yesterday. The bushy-haired one, the art teacher, was a comedian, for he had a way of saying things that made his companion and Abdullah laugh. I laughed, too, because while I couldn't follow exactly what he was saying, I knew that he was talking about our driver. Screwing up his face to mimic the young man's self-importance, and spreading his arms to give himself elbow room, the way our driver had done, he mimicked perfectly his announcement that he would *shugl* (work). That the driver was black was a fact commented on.

While Arabians are not racists (compared to us they are color blind), being black is considered a misfortune. "Zeyd," wrote Doughty, "was a swarthy nearly black sheykh of the desert. . . . So dark a colour is not well seen by the Arabs, who . . . think it resembles the ignoble blood of slave races; and therefore even crisp and ringed hair is a deformity in their eyes." Blacks *were* slaves here—Arabians engaged in the Red Sea slave trade since the beginning of time—and were freed finally by the late King Faisal only in 1962. When teaching my students the names of the basic colors, one of them (dangerously dark himself, but Semitic) was sure to point to a black student in the class and blurt out the obvious: "Awadh—black!" And Awadh, the black student, would be discomfited. The point is that no black student ever pointed to himself with the proud discovery that he was "black." It is curious that the only female faces that go unveiled are the black ones, vendors in the souk of salted dried watermelon and sunflower seeds, which they sell from a shallow straw basket carried on their heads. Students used to brag to me that black

women could be picked up in the souk and taken out to the desert for a little *zug-zug*, but I always thought that this was only wishful fantasizing in the desperate celibacy of their womanless lives.

❖

Abdullah yawned and announced that it was time for a break. At midmorning we were driving through very pretty but desert-dry and very rugged desert-mountain country of travel-poster quality, actually a kind of tableland or front porch to that range of high mountains still ahead of us. At the top of that escarpment sat the sister towns of Abha and Khamis Mushayt. Up there, I hoped, in some hidden valley, some wrinkle in time, I'd find my free, splendid, pre-Islamic woman. On every likely site—a defensible height—were those clusters of abandoned houses built up so carefully of the flags and chips of dark brown native stone, now crumbling away, the fallen pieces spreading out from the foundations like skirts. Abdullah went on playing the guide, touching my arm and silently pointing. He was pleased by my obvious enthusiasm.

"Are those *gadeem* [old], Abdullah?"

"Ough! *Gadee*-eem! [Very old indeed!]" But Saudis have no clear notion of the age of things. Two hundred years is a long span for them. Whenever Abdullah wanted to emphasize antiquity he would raise his finger and twirl it counterclockwise once or twice to indicate, I suppose, backward motion of time. When I pointed out that the old work, so careful, so well wrought, was superior to the new, he agreed: "*Wallah, shugl masboot* [good work]." When Doughty was traveling in Nejd he had a companion named Abdullah too: "We found upon this higher ground potsherds and broken glass. . . . We dismounted, and Abdullah began to say, 'Wellah, the Arabs (of our time) are degenerate

from the ancients, in all!—we see them live by inheriting their labours' (deep wells in the deserts and other public works)!"

I was dying to ask Abdullah about the Legend: how certain of the Arabs in these parts give a sojourning traveler one of their widows for three nights. But as I didn't know how well my unsubtle Arabic could convey my meaning, or how he would receive my question whether garbled *or* plain (talking to them about their women is always risky!), I was afraid to try. But every hour we drove brought us deeper into the country where, according to John Burckhardt, a Swiss who traveled here at the beginning of the nineteenth century, that custom out of paganism prevailed. It sounded, of course, too good to be true, every male traveler's daydream. Burckhardt, who risked his life by reaching Mecca as a disguised Muslim, did not mention the widow. He wrote that in the "Merekede" tribe in "southwest Arabia" (no name like that, alas, on my tribal map, although that's where we were) the host carried out his obligation to be generous by offering the guest his *wife*. This could be a blessing if she were pretty and pleasant, but what if she weren't? And there was another catch: the guest had to "render himself agreeable" to her. If he did, he was treated in the morning "with honor." But if he didn't, the hostess would "cut off the bottom part of his cloak," and the poor impotent wretch would be driven away by pot-banging women and children.

At a primitive *gahhwa* at the roadside we stopped for tea. In the open cooking shed—nothing but a waist-high stone hearth—a round-bottomed aluminum cooking container shaped like an amphora lolled sideways on a bed of coals. The handle of a long wooden spoon stuck out of its narrow, bean-encrusted neck. In this they cook *fool* (beans). There was the pleasant smell of woodsmoke in the dry, hot mountain air. We went under the thatch roof and sat on battered *shai* benches, their woven rope

seats in raveled disrepair. Directly overhead in the open-fronted, low-roofed hovel a leg of mutton, glazed in the dry breeze, hung from the wooden beam by a string. Catching me looking at it, Abdullah said it would keep that way for days.

The man who brought our tea (the usual quart aluminum pot and four little glasses with handles, like miniature beer mugs) was a dried-up shrimp of a Beduin with a stringy gray beard, a hawk's nose, and bare dirty feet. His calves, which showed below his work-stained Yemeni-style skirt, were skinny as a girl's. He immediately wanted to know about me. "What's that?" he demanded of Abdullah, clearly holding him responsible for bringing me there. "*Amreekee,*" was the reply. He looked at me long and thoughtfully. He was a scruffy character, with beady, wild eyes. Fifty years ago I would not have trusted my life with him. Doughty was always running into this type, who threatened, with wicked hissings, to kill him if they found him unprotected. And why? Because he was not a Muslim, because they coveted his few possessions, and because, since he had no tribe to avenge his death "blood for blood," they could get away with it. Once, when Doughty was really in danger, he grabbed a morsel of food that his would-be slayer happened to be eating and ate it—for the bond of "bread and salt" between them, good for twenty-four hours, until the body voided the food. But times have changed, and for that I had to thank the first generation of Sauds who made, through the early application of ruthless capital punishment, and have kept—by the continuing fear of more—this notorious old land of brigands and cutthroats the safest place on earth today. So I wished him peace: "*Salaam aleykum.*" "*Aleykum salaam,*" he replied readily, then sat down with us! Actually I shouldn't have been—and wasn't—surprised. He did leave after a while, after he had satisfied his curiosity, but he did not with-

draw with the idea of giving us privacy. That would never have occurred to him. On the desert there is no privacy. Neither would it have occurred to him to sidle around in a deferential or servile manner. No, Arabian society at its best is wonderfully egalitarian, with a directness and simplicity unknown in the more hierarchical Western democracies.

Abdullah reached to pour me another cup of tea, but I stopped him.

"Only two cups? I drink tea . . . ough! . . . by the potful."

I was thinking how good a cold *beer* would taste, but I remembered that some Saudis I used to know (American-educated, movers in elite circles, drinkers of smuggled Scotch) claimed that to open the door to alcohol would be to insure a zero population growth, for every young Saudi male with a new Japanese car (that meant practically every one of them) and a bellyful of booze would kill himself. To tell the truth, when I lived here and had to drive to work every morning, it was like getting sucked into a wild Bump-a-Car ride. I was glad that the deadly melee was not compounded by legal drunkenness. But could it be much worse? Despite large signs warning drivers of the proper negotiating speed, the concrete embankment of every bad curve we came to for the next hour, from that *gahhwa* to Muhayl, looked like the narrow streets of a German town that Patton's tanks had just battled through. And the road was only two years old! On the asphalt itself, just as the curve began, would be written the desperate signs of panic, long screeching exclamation marks from so many cars making the same reckless miscalculation that in places the whole roadway was black with rubber, and then, *bang!*— every foot of the concrete bank was gouged, cracked, pitted, chipped, and scratched, and bore multicolored striae. After a while such graphic evidence of primitive man in miserable struggle with a modern machine became downright funny. Abdullah asked me what I was smiling about.

"All these *majnoon* [crazy] drivers."

"*Aiwah!* [That's right!] Saudi *majnoon*," he agreed, grinning at my use of that word. "*Ma fee mohkh* [No brains at all]," he added proudly.

We reached Muhayl at eleven o'clock. Why this small cross-roads hill town with an old Turkish stone fort on a promontory was not marked on my map while those insubstantial beehive villages were, is a mystery. Not that its absence or presence on a map printed in England could matter the slightest to anybody except to me. (Nobody ever follows these maps; foreigners use them to decorate a wall.) It was from here that I would take another taxi, according to our driver yesterday, to Abha—but could such a scatterbrain be trusted to get anything right, even this information?

Abdullah stopped his Land Cruiser on the shoulder of the road to let the Egyptians out. I had the feeling that he meant to continue down that road, and could probably have deposited the Egyptians in the very village where they taught "science" and "art," but that he preferred to go on alone. I think the Egyptians sensed it too, because they hinted that although the deal we had made terminated here, they would willingly pay him more to keep going. But Abdullah was vague in his answer. But wait—had I heard right? Pay him *more*? Hadn't Abdullah gently spurned, with the back of his hand, my proferred payment at the *gahhwa* where he picked us up? Ah, but I had misunderstood; it was advance payment that he had brushed aside. He did expect the hundred riyals apiece now, and we paid it gladly. I had grabbed hold of my suitcase, ready to jump out too, but Abdullah stopped me, saying he would take me the half kilometer into Muhayl and show me the taxi. So the Egyptians and I stood behind the Land Cruiser to say good-bye.

"*Fi aman allah* [Godspeed]," I said, shaking their hands.

The "English"-speaking one had it all worked out, and what did he come out with so carefully and distinctly? "Well faring," he said promptly and sincerely.

We left them standing by the road with their old suitcases and tied-up boxes. "Good luck!" I called back. They waved. I felt another pang of pity for these two decent, unselfish, gentlemanly fellows. Unable to make a living in their impoverished country, they had to exist in exile among villagers near Jizan. Most primary and secondary schoolteachers in the kingdom are Egyptians and Jordanians, innocent and unworldly men much like these. They can be had cheap and they fend for themselves on the economy, unlike the pampered and helpless Americans (with more valuable skills) who must be cared for hand and foot. Nothing but an accident of citizenship gave me my privileged, unearned position in the world. (And Abdullah too! What an irony of oil, that a *Saudi's* passport is coveted!) Not that I would give up mine to change places with them. But it certainly wasn't fair.

Muhayl. Muhayl! (I thought I had reached the end of the known world at Kidwat al-Awaj!) A little town somewhere in southwest Arabia, Arabia Exotica, an area almost blank on the world's consciousness *and* its map, and what do I see? A blue-and-white sign announcing Muhayl, in English and Arabic, as nonchalantly as if we were speeding past the turnoff to Cleveland on Interstate 90. Not only that, but we drove right into it on smooth asphalt, so new you could smell the sun-heated tar. I half expected to see that heraldic totem you find on the outskirts of every American town on the older highways, the signs that list the various church denominations, the Rotary Club, the Chamber of Commerce, and so forth. What a windfall for the American company that got the contract to make all those signs! Every little cluster of houses has one—the project, no doubt, of some American-educated Saudi Ph.D.—and they're necessary, I suppose, in order for this last part of Arabia Incognita to reveal herself to the world.

Abdullah stops behind a dirty Toyota Land Cruiser parked in front of a low-roofed *gahhwa*, tells me that that is the taxi and the station, and sticks out his hennaed hand. He'd had a windfall of sorts too, three paying hitchhikers. After a simple, unceremonious good-bye (Arabians make much ado over their greetings, with gracious handshaking and nose-kissing and drawn-out salutations, but are strangely abrupt in their farewells), I get out and Abdullah drives off.

In the hot forenoon there was no shade for my ragless (and hairless) head except that *gahhwa* filled with small, dark men, but I didn't want to crowd in among them just yet. They were a hard-looking bunch, for one thing, and I needed some respite from having constantly to understand and express myself in Arabic. But it didn't matter, for one of them came out to me. He was a thin, middle-aged man wearing a khaki bush jacket over his gray *thobe*—white, in this higher, cooler air, wasn't the automatic choice of color—and he asked me *"ush tib'rah,"* what did I want. He was the driver of that Land Cruiser taxi, a vehicle splashed with dirt like a hog from its wallow, and he told me that everybody was going to eat soon.

"When will we leave?"

"Right after. Maybe half an hour." (That could mean at least an hour.) He took a dirty folded envelope out of his jacket pocket and a ballpoint pen and handed them to me.

"Name," he said.

I printed my name. What could those Roman characters, so distinct, columnar, and blunt-seeming compared to the connected horizontal flow of Arabic, and yet curiously similar to Sabean and the old writing on this peninsula, mean to him? Just as those letters stood out awkward and foreign next to the Abdullahs and Ahmeds on that scrap of envelope, so did I among them. "What does it say?" I pronounced it for him. Repeating the barbaric sounds to himself under his breath, he wrote in Arabic under it as if translating a rude hieroglyphic. "Come eat," he said then. Hoping that wasn't an order (it wasn't quite an invitation, either), I said I wasn't hungry (not true!) and would walk around a bit. He lifted my suitcase—I kept my shopping bag—onto the rack among others, and hurried back under the palm-thatched roof to amuse himself with garrulity. In idle chatter an Arabian will happily while the day away.

Passing a rotisserie of skewered grease-dripping chickens next to the *gahhwa* (the lunch they were all waiting for, obviously), I entered a *dukkan* next door to buy Najran water. I *was* hungry, but not for anything out of that rotisserie, with its undrained well of reheated chicken fat making blue smoke in the hot, still air. Recapping the Najran water after drinking, I dropped it into my shopping bag and crossed over to the souk, where I saw clumps of bananas forked over knotted strings at the vegetable stalls. The souk was only three or four dusty lanes, lined with stalls made of scraps of wood and tin. The narrow space between the stalls was spanned by irregular boards; pieces of canvas, cardboard, and tin (held down by old tires) were placed there to provide shade. The stall where I stopped was kept by a boy of ten.

"How much, the bananas?"

"Five riyals a kilo."

"I only want one. How much?"

"One riyal."

I protested at the robbery, but not seriously, handed him a riyal, and tore a banana (with a Somalia sticker on it) away from its fellows. The boy hesitated only a second before handing me another one, but it was bruised, and from an inferior bunch! How quickly he has learned the shifty dishonesty of his father's trade! I ate the one and then the good half of the mushy other one right there, dropping the peels at my feet. A little girl, the boy's sister perhaps, wearing a purple dress dragging in the dust and four little 21-carat gold bracelets on her arm, looked long at me with her large black eyes. An exotic little thing! And with no shyness in her at all. To my mind, the Semite is a beautiful race, as uniform as a netful of slim, bright sardines, with fewer imperfections per capita than any race I know. By "Semite" I do not include the European Jews of Israel, but the dark, narrow-headed, straight-nosed, small-boned people from the south of Arabia, thought to be the original home of the Semite. Neither do I include the other Arabs, the Egyptians, Palestinians, Syrians, and Iraqis, for these people have been overrun, conquered, mixed with other genes, usually of a coarser sort, and you are as apt to see the broad-faced, heavy-jawed Turkic or Caucasian face among them as the smaller, more symmetrically boned Semite.

I walked the lanes of the little souk, sniffing hungrily of the smells that often, in the antiseptic order of an American supermarket, I have longed for: a peculiar, uniquely Arabian essence compounded of sandalwood, sewage, cumin, leather, rosewater, cardamom, and dust. Across the way a farmer in a soiled *thobe* was selling long white radishes with green tops from a damp burlap bag on the ground. A dog limped along on three legs, its left foreleg nothing but a dangling bone that a piece of wire, twisted into its puppy flesh, had withered. This dog had been leading a hobbling, fugitive life as a souk-scavenger for who knew how long, and nobody paid the slightest attention to its plight. In fact the boyish cruelty had probably been enacted in some slack-jawed moment of midday mindlessness in full apathetic view of *gahhwa* loafers, and dogs count for so little that nobody had prevented it then or remedied it later. *Allah kareem!* God will provide. Farther away, an old gray horse, turned out by its owner, came on its stiff last legs to drink from some puddles among the stone flags where a big brass public water tap dripped. Boys came there with plastic pails to fill for their houses. Here also were a couple of wiry Yemeni water carriers—a dozen years ago a common sight but now very rare—who trotted their balanced full buckets to older houses that didn't have the pump-fed tank on the roof, or lacked an idle boy or prepubescent girl to send for water. The skylarking ragamuffin boys chased and pelted the bewildered old horse for their sport. Turning quickly on the slippery stones to get away, it fell heavily on its side (it has *burst* something, I thought) and lay there struggling to get up. A couple of the water carriers, whether in kindness or because it was in their way, unshouldered their yokes (a split of bamboo, carried rounded-side down) and, shouting encouragement, pulled and pushed until the horse found its feet and blundered half-blind and confused right into the path of a hard-braking Toyota pickup. Such is the well-known fatalism of the Muslim. The idea of "putting it out of its misery" would never occur to them. Doughty had noticed the same thing: "The decrepid dam they abandoned to die, and cut her off from water. As I lay awake I saw her return by night and smell miserably to the water skins in the tent. . . . I asked the Arabs, 'Wherefore not end her lingering pain with a gun-shot?' I thought them cruel, but they thought my words such, and outlandish!"

While I watched these things, enough time had gone by that I thought I should get back to the *gahhwa*. Besides, that torrid sun, having little atmosphere to beat through at this elevation, and finding every other head prudently ragged, took out its frustration on mine. That *gahhwa* was the only shade unless you counted the covered souk lanes, but a recent prayer call, and midday hunger, had emptied them. And even though theft is so rare that a shopkeeper has only to draw a gauzy curtain when he goes off to the mosque to pray, I didn't want to be seen lurking suspiciously therein, a lone *hawaja* among the curtained booths.

A few of the slowest eaters were just finishing their meals (a half of one of those chickens, cleaved in two and served on a heap of yellow rice on a tin tray), but the rest had washed their hands and lolled back to smoke and drink tea, their feet tucked under them on the bench, their sandals or flip-flops on the dirt beneath. The driver waved me inside and I sat down directly across from a very dirty fellow with a grain of moist yellow rice stuck in his kinky beard. He stared at me with goat-yellow eyes. Speaking of goats, a couple of them wandered in and then out, as did a trio of chickens looking for fallen grains of rice, and a skinny cat looking for bones. Arabians stare as frankly as children. There's nothing I could do about it—I couldn't *hurry* the process—so I just sat and waited for them to drink their fill of me, so to speak. In fact all eyes are now on the *hawaja*. Conversations stop. Wanting to be doing something while this inspection is going on (besides *pose* for them), I took out my black shag and my Drum cigarette papers and rolled a cigarette. My neighbor, looking on and nodding as if impressed by my dexterity, borrowed my matches. Our hands touched. He was vile-looking, with not the wholesome grime on him that came from house-building or field work, but from lazing all day in some dirty place. After he took a Craven "A" cigarette out of his box and lit it, he poured from his made-in-Taiwan thermos a lukewarm liquid, cloudy as the Mississippi and with one or two small solid objects making slow suspenseful revolutions in it. This tea, in a smudged glass, he offered to me. I refused. He offered it again. "*Huth* [Take]," said he, and, as politely as I could, with my ingratiating Third World smile and a lie about my stomach, I refused again. He did not seem offended; perhaps it was only a gesture, anyway, and he was relieved that I'd had enough sense to refuse. After that, conversations (animated shouting) resumed. I had been sized up, cataloged, and put away.

A round-faced young man with whom I was sharing the bench tapped my shoulder and asked me what I was: "Omani?"

"No, American."

"America big?"

"Yes, big."

He told me that he studied English sometimes in the evening with an Egyptian (another one of those poor expatriates!). I asked the pleasant-faced young man what *bilad* this was. He wrote on the palm of his hand in blue ballpoint—he would not say the names—and showed me:

ASIRY

GAHTANI

I try some English on him: "Is your teacher good?"

"Yes . . . good."

"Does he speak English the way I speak it?"

"Yes . . . he speak English."

"I mean does he . . . wait, never mind. Uh"—I poked my chest—"I, English teacher too."

"You! Teacher!"

"Yes. Look. If I came to Muhayl—"

"You . . . come Muhayl?"

"No." (Back to Arabic.) "If I came to Muhayl and opened a school, a *madrasah Eengleesee*, could I make money?"

"Ough! *Kul' idduniyah* [everybody, literally 'all the world'] wants to learn English. I want English so I can go to Jidda and open a business."

"Why Jidda? Why not here?"

"Here is nothing. What is here? Jidda is where the life is." (The illusion of every yearning provincial soul: convinced that life is "there" and that "here" is the backwardest of backwaters.)

To be fair, Muhayl wasn't exactly in the swim of things, and when the driver finally rose to go, I was ready. The best seats were taken in a quick scramble, leaving the two fold-down seats in the very back for me. When we were all in place the driver asked for my fare—fifty riyals—and my passport. The rest had already paid, apparently. I gave it to him, but he couldn't read the numbers on my passport, so I called them out in Arabic while he wrote in a book. But then he had to take it inside the *gahhwa* and copy the numbers, laboriously and without the sense of it, just as I would have to copy Arabic. When he came back with my passport he took, not insolently but without asking, either, a swig of my water. Then he slammed the back door on me, locked the handle, and yelled *Yallah!*—Let's go! But he is stopped at the last second by the shout of a huge black *Sudanee*, immaculate in eye-dazzling white, who hurries up miffed that he was about to be left behind. The only place for this giant is in the back with me. After first banging the dusty seat, he climbs, complaining of the dirt, into the cramped space. We fit by me putting my legs one way, he scrunching his another. Now, after sighing and settling himself like a hot engine put into idle, he proceeds to take me in slowly and by stages, as they all do, like a snake swallowing a rabbit, from my red scalp down to my dirty bare feet. He has enormous dignity as he sits there like a huge

African king. Somewhere in the folds of his Egyptian-style galabia he finds a white handkerchief and mops the sweat off the shiniest, biggest, blackest face I have ever seen. *Sudanees* do not wear their headrags in the Saudi style, folded to make a triangle and then simply draped over their skullcaps, but fix them somehow in loose white billows. He was wearing black leather shoes and a large silver ring, crudely worked. I caught him noticing my gold filigree one, then he looked out the window and fingered his own absentmindedly.

We climbed toward the mountains, and if I'd known what I was in for, I'd have flown, or walked. All went fine for twenty minutes as we sped along new blacktop through landscape that was . . . well, nearly bucolic: those stone houses and towers, some crumbling and some inhabited; those narrow strips and patches of cultivation; that escarpment that we had somehow to get to the top of. It was just great, and as the big *Sudanee* and I looked past each other out the side windows, and out the back at each receding "village" as we climbed higher into the wadi, I got that sensation of well-being that comes over the tourist when everything is going well. I rolled a cigarette without spilling a shred as we hummed smoothly along, and exhaled self-congratulatory smoke into the eddyless air. I took a swig from my water bottle after first offering it to that black statue in the white sheet, but he either didn't like the look of me, or he wasn't thirsty, for he declined with a grave shake of his massive head. A little below us (our fold-down seats were on a higher level), the three rows of small Semitic heads, each covered with a rag (they did not wear the twisted black rope, the *egal*, that foppish affectation of the town-Arabian), appeared, as they sat with their narrow shoulders hunched to accommodate each other, like nine old ladies wearing shawls. How they found the room to do it I don't know, but each one of them chain-smoked cigarettes. When the Wahhabis (Islamic fanatics) banned tobacco, on the assumption that Mohammed wouldn't have liked it, what suffering there must have been!

But then the driver pulls over onto the shoulder of the road, then slows to a man's walking speed as he turns smack into a dry stream bed, a thorn-tree-filled and rock-strewn wadi! As the *Sudanee* and I began bouncing around, holding on to our seats to keep from banging our heads, we searched each other's eyes in concerned surmise. "*Esh hatha?* [What's this?]" he called to the driver, who was fighting the wheel as he eased into gullies and over rocks. "I want to go to Abha."

"This is the road to Abha. Shortcut."

"How long is this shortcut?" I asked in alarm.

"Only a hundred kilometers," one of the men in front answered, looking back as he grinned so that I saw a flash of gold.

"What!"

"Only a joke. We will be on this road for only an hour, *inshallah* [God willing]. The asphalt road takes three."

I'd have preferred a smooth three hours to this one-hour shaking up, but as I had no say in the matter (I couldn't even open the door and get out), I hung on with both hands. Arabians have no proportion in their lives. They will laze a day away in a *gahhwa*, but when they do get going it is all rush and hurry and impatience to get there. I learned later, from my friend Bob, that there are several vertical "roads" right up the escarpment, ancient camel trails, roughly scraped to allow hardy vehicles, but as everybody wanted to use them to "save" two hours (with the inevitable result that some drivers bought a lot more time than they'd counted on), the plan is to make them safer and asphalt them. Perhaps it has been done by now, but I don't care. Engineering and paving that road now can't restore to me the years it took off my life, the gray hairs it added to my head. The escarpment has some of the wildest, ruggedest mountain-scape in the world, and there I was, as big a fool as any (bigger! I was locked in) crawling straight up it, sealed in a vehicle with nine *fatalists*! I think if I had known what was yet to come I would have gotten right out and hitched the long way to Abha. I have to give credit to that Land Cruiser and its driver, however; we never faltered when our wheels were only inches from thousand-foot drops. As we hairpinned and switchbacked our way up, crossing from ridge to valley to ridge, chatter stopped. On and on we ground our way upward. Often, at particularly steep or rough places, the driver had to stop completely, brake to keep from rolling back (or off!), and shift into four-wheel drive. Worse yet, he had to *reverse* a foot or two to get it out of four-wheel drive, a peculiarity of that vehicle that, the first time it happened, I heart-stoppingly interpreted as brake failure. In some level places water was still standing after recent showers, and in others, gullies had washed the declivity side of the "road"—a few scraped feet of bare mountain rock—away. Then the driver had to take more of the mountainside to gain purchase for his wheels, and in those spots we tilted dangerously. The heavy *Sudanee* was on the listward side, too, and I was afraid my slight weight was not compensating ballast. If I had flown, I could not help reminding myself, I would not be sitting here with nothing but air and rubber and a foot of crumbly rock between me and destruction. In case I needed reminders of what carelessness or technical failure (a blowout! brakes!) could lead to, I saw, during the course of our climb, four vehicles smashed to pieces far down in deep ravines and distant ledges. Their occupants had not received decent burial, either, for there was simply no way to get down to them. When the

Sudanee and I happened to be looking out the back window at the same time, and saw the first one, our eyes met. After a little he began softly chanting a sura, and composed himself stoically for the end.

But the view was beautiful, so I tried to forget my fear of sudden death and take it in. Delicate grass with silver heads blew in the upland breeze in shimmering waves like wheat, but otherwise, except for some stunted bushes, and tiny desert-mountain wildflowers, the great steep slopes were bare of trees.

After an hour we reached the top, and at nine thousand feet entered another world. Here suddenly were terraced fields of wheat, steep fields terraced right up to the top of every cleft and cleavage where there was a little soil, and rain-chilled air. There, white on its barren brown hills (I thought of San Francisco) was Abha; we had come up to it by its backyard, so to speak. Still none of us had said a word. In fact we had been a very silent, solemn, nervously smoking group on the way up. As we took our last bump—onto smooth asphalt, for they had paved out from Abha this far, then stopped—and experienced the immense relief that went with it, a happy arrow of wit formed in my mouth and I shot it into the heavy silence: "*Mabrouk!* [Congratulations!]." There was an explosion of delighted laughter as all heads turned to look at the *hawaja*. With that one word, I had bought more goodwill for my countrymen than a million dollars of propaganda.

At a wadi, which was running across the road with shallow water (but running, in riverless Arabia!), we stopped. Some of the men went off a ways and squatted; three, including the *Sudanee*, knelt to pray. I got out, shivering in my sweat-stiffened cotton shirt, and watched a stocky old man, wearing a sports jacket over his *thobe* and a Pakistan-made wool *ghutra* on his head, keeping herd on a flock of goats grazing on the steep hillside. He did this by throwing rocks in front of them to head them off when they strayed too far, and by making a high *skirr* deep in his throat. With obvious pleasure, and tender chidings, this jut-bearded patriarch humored a granddaughter at his feet who threw pebbles in awkward imitation of his accurate chuckings. The girl's hair was as black as the crows that flew over the terraced half-moons of wheat; here and there, set up to frighten them, stood *thobes*-on-sticks. She wore a red, long-sleeved gown, and her little henna-dyed feet were bare. Arabian women have a heartbreaking beauty, and it is easy to understand why a jealous patriarchy, covetous and possessive, would want to hide such treasures from potential thieves (meaning, of course, every man not in the immediate family).

The driver, who did not pray, watched the three who did with impatience. Wanting to be on his way, he muttered something impolite and then called out, "*Yallah!* [Let's go!]," not specifically to them (impiety!) but to us all. But they were not to be hurried. Just as yesterday I had discovered that I didn't know what thirst was until I experienced dehydration in the Jimps, so now, looking at those men with their foreheads on the ground and their butts up in the air, I realized that although I had observed thousands of men in that position over the years, I had never really *seen* it. Allah, it is said, revealed to Mohammed, who then taught it to his followers, this peculiar way that He liked to be worshiped. It is also reported that Allah wanted the Arabians to do this *fifty* times a day (either as a way of keeping them out of trouble, or to abase them for that long binge of arrant paganism), but Mohammed, sorry for his neighbors (and there were goats to be milked!), interceded and got it cut down to five. (If I were a Muslim I'd pray to *him.*) No, all that abject bowing and scraping predated Mohammed, and is identical, in fact, to the salaaming postures that slaves used to approach Oriental potentates. As I stood there in the Arcadian-sweet, rain-washed, almost alpine air, and watched those men go through their motions, I knew that if Mankind was a horse in a race I wouldn't bet on it.

PART TWO

ARABIA FELIX

❖

CHAPTER FOUR

The Compound;
Zahran

A welcome drink. Shangri-la. Najran water contaminated.
"Concrete curtain" between Americans and Saudis. A rock
carving. Poking around in the souk. I "steal" a rug. Food.
Souk-Arabia. "Wild men" of old Asir. Taxi fixed up like a
boudoir. A *muttawa*. A hair-cutting. Roadside graffiti. Reforestation efforts. Plastic "leaves." The worst road in the world.
Arabia Incognita.

I wasn't in such need of a bath as Thesiger was when he crossed
the Empty Quarter (I was more in need of a sidiki and tonic),
but I relished it (and the drink) all the same. As much as I
looked forward to hot water and cold spirits, I wanted a little
privacy, the chance to relax and catch my breath in my own
language and habits of mind, to get away from Arabs for a while;

and all this I found at Bob's house in the Khamis Mushayt "can-
tonement," as the Americans call their walled housing compound.

Bob had quite a comfortable setup in Shangri-la: a new three-
bedroom house, a backyard of grass and castor bean bushes that
he had coaxed out of gravel with a lawn sprinkler and American-
made chemical fertilizers bought in the souk (along with the grass
seed). At sundown we'd drink "squeak" (*sidiki,* the local moon-
shine) and charcoal-grill frozen steaks from the States or frozen
chicken from Romania while Bob moved his sprinkler from place
to place. From his patio we could look out over a good part of
the square-mile compound. Attached to an air base a few kilometers from Khamis Mushayt, Abha's twin city, its neat layout
of paved streets and cement sidewalks and cars parked at the
curbs reminded me, were it not for a concrete wall dividing the
compound into two halves, of a suburb of Tucson, Arizona. Bob's
next-door neighbors, a young flight-line mechanic from Texas
and his towheaded wife, had a boat on a trailer in the carport
which they hauled down behind a pickup truck to the Red Sea
on weekends. TV cable ran from roof to roof, connecting the
flat-roofed houses in a kind of tribal closed circuit, and in every
living room sat a company-supplied Sanyo, showing silent an-
nouncements of company and community business until the late
afternoon, when the evening's entertainment (hours of taped
American TV, commercials and all) would begin.

"Shadows on the cave's wall," said Bob. After six years in "this
luxurious jail," as he called it, he had reached that stage of
burnout and boredom that not even a week's holiday in heaven—
much less the usual getaway to Cyprus—could cure. For myself,
I was very unhappy to read, my first day here in Arabia the
Happy, one of those white messages on the blue screen: A RECENT
SAMPLE OF NAJRAN BOTTLED WATER WAS FOUND TO BE GROSSLY

CONTAMINATED. DO NOT DRINK UNTIL FURTHER NOTICE. *Grossly* contaminated! Did a Beduin squat over the well, or what? Now, that's the kind of news that makes you want to stay home. Had I come back to Arabia, then, to carry away in my gut some lifelong amoebic reminder (I'd already had severe hepatitis here, a feces-borne disease of the liver) of Arabia Excrementa? Worse yet, not only had I been guzzling Najran bottled water with abandon for two days, but Bob had just used a bottle of it to cut our stock of hard-to-get bootleg sidiki. Now *that* was a dilemma. Should we throw it out? "Let's hope the alcohol kills the bugs," Bob decided like a true Third World hand, quartering limes for a couple of fresh drinks.

Although Bob led a perfectly comfortable life (and less boring than that lived by millions of Americans, for that matter), it wasn't enough. As he put it, "If I get to heaven and find that there's no New York City or fresh mozzarella cheese, I'm gettin' the hell out!" He had given the company ninety days' notice, sent his wife and child home, and was, when I arrived, "batching it, bored, horny, marking time, and counting money," waiting impatiently for me, in fact, so that we could go "bashing the boonies" together in his canvas-topped Toyota Land Cruiser for one last fling in Arabia Antigua. The high point we had planned was the wedding of one of our former students, off in some lost village at the very edge of the escarpment. "Talk about primitive Arabia! Man, we'll be the first white men to set foot in this place! Those fuckers sing and dance and leap like savages in the firelight, waving swords and shooting off rifles! And, hey, if we don't find your horny pre-Islamic widow back in *them* hills, you can forget her!" Bob was the reddest person I had ever seen— red hair, red eyebrows, red freckles. He was also a good host and a cheerful traveling companion, and what more could you ask of anybody?

As soon as we recovered from our hangovers we started right in on the local sights of the *new* Arabia, beginning with the compound. Down the middle a "concrete curtain," seven feet high, divided Saudi from American, Muslim from Christian. There was no intercourse between them. Four years before, when the compound was new (the government had crash-expanded an air base and stationed a squadron of newly purchased F-5 fighters to defend its southern border against any threat from its Marxist neighbor, the People's Democratic Republic of Yemen), it was, according to Bob, "wide open when I got here—boogieing all night, sidiki, dope, even some Saudi *wives* at parties. Can you believe it?" But the inevitable occurred. There was a tiny minority who couldn't handle such liberty (there always is). Instead of taking those aberrant members "out to a vacant lot and shooting them," as Bob suggested, the vast majority, who could tolerate higher doses of freedom, were punished for the crimes of those few. Because of them, visiting between the compounds was discouraged. All that could be seen on the Muslim side by the nonbeliever's eye was the top half of a small pointed minaret topped by the usual quarter moon (this one of shining brass) and a loudspeaker. But what the mosque lacked in size it made up for in volume, for its clarion calls to prayer five times a day stunned the ear of believer and nonbeliever alike. This wall is sad proof that the fundamentalist sort of Islam practiced in Arabia has to pull itself in, like a snail, to protect itself. But what is it they are so determined to protect? This "fool's paradise," as Doughty called the Islam he found here ("But I could not find it in my life to confess the barbaric prophet of Mecca and enter, under the yoke, into their solemn fool's paradise"), is hardly some precious artifact in danger of being crushed by contact with a crass outside world. Islam does not make men any better than any other religion. Because the fundamentalist version of it keeps them insulated, exclusive, fanatical, and ignorant, it makes them worse.

❖

Bob wanted to show me a rock carving, so we drove a few miles out on the Najran road. We climbed up a cinder cone about the size and slope of the Great Pyramid, and near the top we came to a rock overhang, a natural shelter frequented, apparently, by early man and present-day baboons. Bob had seen a pack of baboons there a week earlier, and as we entered I smelled their strong zooey odor and saw dung fresh enough to make me nervous. But sure enough, scratched shoulder-high in the wind-worn hollow of rock, were two figures of gazelles, now nearly extinct in Arabia; Thesiger reported in 1945 that royal hunting parties "scour the plains in cars, returning with lorry-loads of gazelle which they have run down and butchered." As we stood in the wind at the porch of the cave, two swifts, nearly close enough to grab, came to ride and cavort in the strong dry thermal. The sleek birds probably couldn't tell us from the baboons. From this height Bob pointed to another cinder cone in the distance and indicated that this was the place where Solomon met the Queen of Sheba, according to the Koran. If that's true, my Sunday school teachers were wrong. According to the color illustrations of Bible scenes that were handed out to us innocent, suffering children in those boxlike Sunday school rooms, the Queen of the South journeyed up from Yemen (ancient Sabea, or Sheba) to visit Solomon in Jerusalem. It doesn't matter a fig to anybody whether they met at that pile of rocks or another, or even if they met at all. What *is* interesting, or would be to the women of this peninsula if they learned something of their past besides what they are required to memorize from the Koran, is that the land of Sheba was a pagan queendom. (And one of her descendants, I hoped, was that hospitable widow I hoped to meet.)

❖

While Bob was at work I amused myself by doing what I liked best, and it's the only thing a foreigner *can* do here, since there are no movies, theaters, bars, clubs, museums, monuments, statues, zoos or botanical gardens, exhibitions, libraries, lectures, concerts, or whorehouses: I poked around in the Khamis Mushayt and Abha souks. Most Americans don't like doing this and depend on the compound for every need, but I felt at home in the dirty lanes and alleys around the souk. Anyway, there is nothing else of interest or attraction in an Arabian town.

One day I saw a rug there that gave me such a "rug-on" (as a friend in Taif used to say when he had a strong urge to visit the rug souk) that I thought of stealing it—even though I was in a country where they chopped off your right hand for that. I was thinking of stealing it because I couldn't buy it, and I couldn't buy it because three Pakistanis had, because of me, become aware of it. In other words, I was afraid that if I didn't steal it, they would.

A corner of the rug was visible, only the corner, but the colors, and that portion of the design that I could see, snagged my trolling eye. We notice what interests us. All that the unmotivated eye *sees* are two old rugs, stiff and dirty, lying on top of a broken air conditioner. The one on top, which was folded, faded, and ragged, covered the one I coveted. I approached. From the corner that was visible I imagined the whole, but braced myself for disappointment. How many times have I seen an exciting back of a rug (collecting rugs kept me going during my last contract here) only to turn it over and find . . . To put it another way, suppose you saw the lovely back of a woman and, imagining her front to be equally desirable, you discover her face half eaten away by some disease, her breasts missing, her belly and thighs nothing but scar tissue. This is exactly the case with most old rugs I used to "find," rugs not already in a dealer's shop and hence costing a thousand dollars. Repeated disappointments don't, however, deter the true collector (of women or of old rugs). Nonchalantly, in case the owner was observing me, I took that exposed corner between thumb and forefinger, and lifted. One glance was all I needed. Ravishing. Now . . . was it all there, or was it only a scrap, a half of a rug? I continued lifting. A "tribal" from south Iran, a Kashgai: I caught a glimpse of a white "crab" centerpiece, madder-red field strewn with tiny stylized plants and animals, ethereal-blue corners, multistepped border before the field.

I looked around, my heart racing with larcenous excitement. The noon street, glaring under the Arabian sun, was strangely quiet. Prayer time. Whose rug was it? Suppose I just picked it up and started walking away? If stopped, I could innocently explain that I thought it had been thrown out. After all, it wasn't in anyone's house, it was practically on the street, a place Arabians consider a legitimate dump, there being no other. It was obvious that it wasn't valued. When I moved it I had felt the brittleness of the warp and weft. A good wash with soap and water, a thorough rinse, and a drying under the hot sun would restore much of its suppleness and color, but if someone valued it—as I did—why would he have left it there to the mercy of the elements? To the rain, the sun, and the gritty wind? By now I had almost convinced myself that I deserved it.

I glanced—my guilty thoughts transparent—up and down the "street." (When I say street, I am describing something like a clear space in a rubble-strewn lot, with some cinder-block-walled "villas" plunked down at random.) Should I? Just fold it under my arm and make off? How else to possess it? How could I ever find the owner of this rug? On the other side of the broken air conditioner was a low cinder-block structure, unmortared, that looked like an abandoned shed. It had a small barred window at which, in the comic agony of my irresolution, I unseeing stared. To take it, or not to take it? The longer I stood there like a dummy, the more suspicious and less casually authoritative would my presence seem there. But, dammit, in Saudi Arabia one just doesn't *steal*. Hands are cut off for it. I had seen, in the old days, severed hands, each hanging by its middle finger, turning black in front of the Jidda police station. It's true that I haven't seen any for a long time, but it's because there are fewer thieving hands, and the police have become sensitive about publicly displaying them. (It's a reaction, probably, to the horrified Western press, but it is rare to meet a Westerner *in* Arabia who did not approve of their swift, harsh justice.) What the hell. I was a foreigner. I could always claim ignorance of the law, couldn't I? By now the sweat was pouring guiltily off my face. Or could I? There are foreigners rotting in Saudi jails right now, and they are there because they thought their foreignness gave them immunity.

Then I became aware of a face watching me from behind the bars in that window a few feet from me. It hadn't just popped up there. It had, I realized, been there for some time, but I hadn't seen it because it was as dark as the interior of the shed contrasted to the glare outside where I was standing. I dropped the rug as if I'd been holding a scorpion by the tail.

"*Salaam alaykum* [Peace to you]."

"*Alaykum salaam* [To you peace]." But said unwillingly, and after a long silence.

"*Hatha sujjadah hagguk?* [This rug yours?]"

"*La* [No]."

"*Min?* [Who?]"

His hand swept the air as if to say, "Out there."

"*Wayn?* [Where?]"

He shrugged. This Pakistani, thick as a mud fence, made a shooing motion at me with his hand, as if I had been a chicken or worse, and turned away. Hold on. Just a damned minute! I stepped around the rusty air conditioner and squeezed myself between it and the window, my face to the bars. Now I could see inside the tiny room. Two other men were there, squatting on the dirt floor. I realized that this place was where they lived. I saw a gas bottle and a burner on the sand, a few pots, and "beds." (A bed, in this kind of immigrant-workman's hovel, is a pile of rags.)

"*Hal tabeeyah hatha?* [Want to sell this?]"

"*Moosh hagnah* [Not ours]." One of them stood up and explained that their boss, whose property this was and to whom, presumably, the rug belonged, was in Mecca and would not be back for a few days. Rotten luck for me, I thought.

I covered my rug—I already considered it mine—with the other one. I didn't want it exposed to the sun or to other passersby. I told them I'd come back in a day or two. Nobody answered me. They must have been thinking, Who the hell is this guy? Halfway down the block I looked back. All three of them had come outside. They were staring after me. Then they started looking at my rug. Dammit, it was clear that they hadn't even known it was there.

Well, I had to have that rug, and I thought of little else but how to get it. In fact, if it had been a girl, and that hovel her house, I would have made a fool of myself. I was a lovesick swain. I couldn't stay away. I invented excuses to keep going by. My motives were twofold: I wanted to see the rug, to reassure myself that it was still there; and I wanted to establish in the Pakistanis' heads the fact that I was . . . well, a neighbor, that I was permanent, that I lived close by and came that way often—that, for all they knew, I was a friend of their boss. One day I passed by three times, carrying purchases from the souk as if routinely shopping. The second day I let myself be seen twice. Still there. But then I began to have a new fear as a definite plan for getting the rug emerged in my mind. If at first I regretted that they were not Saudis, men made honest by fear of punishment, now I was glad that they were foreigners, and of questionable honesty. For I saw that the only way of getting it was to buy it from them. It was obvious to me, and I hoped it was becoming obvious to them. Their "boss" didn't give a damn about those old rugs. Anyway, it made no difference if he did, because they only had to shrug and pretend to know nothing if ever asked. If, on the other hand, he came back and was *told* that a foreigner had been inquiring about a rug he hadn't even known about. . . . You should see the glitter in a shopkeeper's eyes when he knows he's got something you want. No, that had to be prevented. I had come full circle, from hoping that they weren't thieves to hoping that they were, and that we could steal this rug together.

Accordingly, I singled out the most intelligent of them: Look, I told him, we have a problem. I worked, and he worked, and his boss worked, and because of our jobs and different hours it could be weeks before we chanced to be together at the same time. I told him I'd be going out of town for a while the day after tomorrow, but that I'd come by again *one last time* (I didn't want to overemphasize it, but I didn't want to chance it slipping by him, either) before I went. Possibly you will have talked to your boss by then, I said, and *if he isn't here* when I come by, *malesh* (never mind), I'll pay *you* the money and you can give it to him. (Was I overdoing this? I hoped not.) Understand? Goodbye, then, until tomorrow at about this time. There. I had made it easy for him, and if he hadn't lost the sense he was born with, we'd both be happier tomorrow.

Now I had only to figure out what he would let the rug go for. When the time came I put four hundred-riyal bills in my left pocket (each hundred riyals is worth twenty-eight dollars) and all my smaller bills, which amounted to forty-seven riyals, in my right. With a few coins, it came to forty-eight riyals, or thirteen dollars and change. I thought that would take it, but in case there really was a boss, and my man was fool enough to drag him into it, I had the extra money in reserve. It was actually "worth" much more than I was carrying, but I doubted that the wildest stab-in-the-dark price the Pakistani would ask, one that would leave him breathless at his presumption, would be much above two hundred, and I was prepared to fight hard if it went beyond that.

On the morrow all three of them came out. I confronted them. "Well, how much does your boss want for this rug?" The spokes-man: "He said you can have it for whatever you think is fair." "Well," I said, "let's see." Hoping that the trembling of my hands wasn't obvious, I took it down for the first time and spread it on the ground for a full look. Luckily, it was very dirty and "looked" awful, but I knew how to see through the dirt. While they watched, I carefully fingered a couple of small holes and let my hand regretfully explore a worn place, and then I stood up and reached into my right pocket like a poker player who has made up his mind to call a raise. I took out the wad of small bills and counted. Ten, twenty, thirty . . . I pretended to pause, to think. One more, forty . . . I paused again. Ah, what the hell. I dug into my pocket again for the change and shoved all of it, everything I had on me (in that pocket), all forty-eight riyals, into the spokesman's blue-black hand, which closed on it like a spider possessing its prey. Do I feel I cheated them? Not at all. One of them, the one who had been so unfriendly four days before, even helped me fold it, then helped me hoist it to my shoulder. He was grinning now. He thought I was the biggest fool who ever lived.

❖

I really knew I was in Arabia Felix (or anyway, at seven thousand feet, Arabia Alta) in the morning. While the rest of the hapless peninsula is already sweating like a chicken on a spit, the covered lanes of the Khamis souk are earthy and cool with fresh damp vegetables, as if they brought with them the night's chill. I would say that on the whole (how Doughty would smite his forehead on hearing this!), the average Arabian eats better than the average American. When Doughty traveled here a century ago, most of the population was among the world's poorest, Beduins living on a scanty diet of dates and camel's milk. Now there are no more Beduins, no more camels to speak of, and no more *hunger,* with the result that whole plantations of date palms in Al-Hasa, near the Gulf, stand neglected and ruined for lack of husbandry, their owners choosing to make money in some more modern way. (If I had a riyal for every hasty sign over every raw cinder-block doorway that read "Ali's Establishment for Trading," or "Ahmed's Import and Export," I'd be a rich man.) They eat well now because everybody has money, the food is there, and they are not yet addicted to junk and "convenience" food. What they don't grow in small hand-tended plots—spinach, chard, purslane, lettuce, parsley, mint, eggplant, okra, tomatoes, potatoes, cucumbers, squash, beans, carrots, turnips, radishes, melons, cactus buds, limited amounts of figs, pomegranates, grapes, lemons, apricots, apples, and walnuts—they import: bananas from Somalia and Ecuador, citrus from Lebanon, black grapes from Sudan, mangoes from India, shiny red apples from Switzerland. (They grow a local apple, but because the fruit is small and imperfect, Arabians prefer the cosmetically superior apples from Europe.) Most of the stalls are kept by men who squat or sit cross-legged among the produce, compulsively and fastidiously arranging it in neat piles and pyramids; but it is not unusual to see unveiled crones wearing the broad-brimmed conical hats they use when working in their tiny "fields." *"Ta'al* [Come]," they called me lazily in their crow's caw. They beckoned to me with a downward motion, as if they were paddling in the water to bring some floating object closer. *"Ta'al shuf* [Come and look]." One, whose palms were dark red with henna, was selling grape leaves from a basket. I walked slowly back and forth, reveling in the old souk-Arabia that I loved. *"Ta'al." "Esh tib'rah?* [What do you want?]" *"Ta'al hinna"* [Come here]." The women sat or reclined on the earth out of the sun in makeshift cardboard hovels no larger than packing crates, dirtying the ground around them by leaning sideways to spit snuff-browned saliva. One had a straw basket of small pullet eggs for which she wanted a riyal apiece. I shook one of the little brown nuggets, "listening" with my fingers for an addled looseness. "He knows," observed a skinny hag in her packing crate only a few feet away, the toenails of her hard-used dirty feet (they had never known shoes) carefully hennaed. One younger woman had an infant nursing at a clean, surprisingly fair breast with a very dark nipple. Her face was veiled. But another one, from whom I bought a half kilo of baby cucumbers for our dinner salad, met my eyes after a minute of playful haggling and held the glance. The glance seemed to say, Well, if things were different. . . .

Then there are the "flower ladies," as Bob charitably called them, barefoot old women selling sprays of mountain herbs, wild thyme and rosemary and flowers with a breath-catching wild fragrance that they make into bouquets or twist into garlands. I never knew what these were used for until the morning when suddenly (as deer will materialize quietly out of nowhere) two "wild men" (as Bob called them) appeared to buy the scented herbs. My pulse quickened, as if I were in the presence of a rare species of animal—which I was. They were clean, handsome youths, not dark, of medium height and perfect, slim build. They stooped, and carefully but quickly made their selections of aromatic weeds. They paid the pittance without haggling, discarded their wilted circlets, and braided the fresh stems quickly into garlands that they wore as scented headbands for their straight black hair. They were completely self-possessed and without self-consciousness. Surely these were the ones my Ghahtani student had told me about: came to town "sometimes" . . . shy, "like animals" . . . from villages far off the beaten paths . . . did not "pray," they were "not Muslims" (and oh, how furious was the fanatical Nejdi on hearing *that*). Yes, these were the ones; I realized I was seeing the "old Arabia," a direct glimpse right into it, like following a shaft of light straight up through a hole in the clouds. These herbal crowns were *pre-*"pre-Islamic"; they were pagan, Hellenic, antique as man at the dawn, in the Golden Age. These long-haired, barefoot men in loincloths had a dignified masculine innocence that skipped three thousand years of human history. They made the Saudi, mincing nearby in his long dress and twirling his car keys nervously like worry beads, seem like a member of a lesser race.

When I looked again for the youths, they were gone. They had disappeared as mysteriously as they had come.

❖

Being footloose in the early morning allowed me to pursue my true and proper vocation, which is to be a tourist and a traveler through life. My notebook went along with me as I copied their words as fresh out of their mouths as possible. As the act of writing (or of reading) is seen rarely, if ever, among the Arabians, it is a subject of curiosity bordering on hostility, as if a secret language were being spoken to their detriment. Because this was somewhat true, it made me guarded and guilty.

"*Esh hatha?* [What's this?]" demanded the young taxi driver, taking the notebook out of my lap to leaf disdainfully through the incomprehensible pages. "What are you writing?" He was driving a Toyota Cressida with a fur-covered dashboard and a curtained back window with gold draw-tassels. A cassette of wild wailing music was blaring, and all the windows were open to admit the buffeting wind. He was smoking in a jerky, nervous way, and his Saudi-gaudy sandal was mashing the accelerator to the floor. He was perfumed. He smelled like a honeysuckle vine on a summer night.

"Letter to my wife."

"Long letter. What are you?" (Arabians want to know everything about you right away.)

"I'm a teacher. In Jidda."

"What are you doing here?"

"Visiting a friend. Easy there, sheikh. Look out for that truck."

"That truck is no problem." *Whoosh!* He sped around it as if it were standing still.

"What's the hurry? I don't want to die before I finish this letter to my wife."

"*Allah kareem* [God is generous]," he said, but he did slow down a little. "Jidda *quais* [good]?"

"*Quais.*"

"Jidda . . . *madame katheee-er* [*lots of women*]." He flipped a corner of his headrag to expose an ear and coils of long black hair. He had such a loose, nervous sexuality, and such a desperate carnal hunger in his blood-flecked, haunted eyes that he reminded me of one of the bewitched buffoons in Shakespeare's comedy.

Dale Walker

I was afraid he'd become violently enamored of any creature who happened to be on the same seat with him.

"*Aiwah* [Yeah]," I agreed, "*madame katheer*. You married?"

"No."

"How do you find women"—I spoke as two men of the world discussing a sexual backwater—"around Khamis?"

"Here, there," he said offhandedly. It would be unmanly to admit that about the only place he came across any sex was in his hand. "On the desert. In your car."

"Really? Which women?"

"*Bedu.*"

This boast of the sharp-faced young lout was nothing but air. Not that all the young men didn't try. Every baffled, horny male in the kingdom (that means every young unmarried man) spends an inordinate amount of time and money decorating his car to look like a boudoir, and then cruising around in it perfumed, handsome, and smug, tape deck playing shrilly, in hope of . . . what? In Texas in the fifties, we teen-agers in our souped-up cars would cruise around and around the town, Hank Williams on the radio, hoping to pick up girls. We seldom did, but we made up for our frustration—we were too young to join the army—by getting into fights with boys in cars from different high schools. Meanwhile, the girls we were hoping to "pick up" were home watching television and being groomed by their mothers for marriage. The hapless Saudi youths (fighting is not an acceptable moral equivalent here) have even less of a chance for a sexual adventure than we did. After all, we were lucky to live within driving distance of the Mexican border and the cathouses there. For the young Saudi there is only imagination and the dogged hope such as inspires the bowerbird to feather, fur, bedazzle, bedeck, and embroider his would-be love nest. *His* success rate, only one in two hundred, cannot be any worse than the Saudi's.

We waited for the red light on the outskirts of Khamis. When traffic lights were introduced in the kingdom (in Al-Khobar and Dammam only a little over a decade ago), it was dangerous to stop if a car was close behind you. Some drivers obeyed them and some didn't, so that the local hospitals were full of whiplash injuries. As we waited, an old man came striding on bare feet in our direction. His patriarch's beard was dyed an unabashed orange, he wore over his *thobe* an open, flowing *bisht* (gold-trimmed finespun woolen cloak), and he carried a stick with authority. Quite an impressive figure.

"Who's he?"

"Who? Him?" He shrugged, ashamed to acknowledge that old relic (as they are sometimes ashamed of their "old things," which we value as antiques) before the *hawaja*. "Nobody. *Muttawa* [Religious police]."

Nobody! *Muttawa!* What had happened here? "He's a nobody?" I teased. "Ten years ago he would have cut off that long hair of yours."

I told him what I had witnessed on the streets of Al-Khobar a decade before. At that time there was a comic pair who patrolled the garbage-fermenting streets of that Persian Gulf town, a giant *muttawa* and his diminutive sidekick, a sergeant in the National Guard, a grotesque duo whom we Americans nicknamed Mutt and Jeff.

One noonday Mutt and Jeff were patrolling in the area of the Al-Khobar vegetable souk when they happened upon a young man, really a handsome, slight boy of about fifteen, inching along with the construction-bottlenecked traffic in his father's Land-Rover. (Since there is no enforced legal driving age, you often see striplings behind the wheel who can barely see over the dashboard.) The boy's hair was not long, it barely covered the tops of his ears; and seemingly having no reason to conceal it, he was innocently wearing only a white skullcap worked in gold thread. Nevertheless, once he was out of the single-file neck of the obstruction (a whole generation of Saudis have grown up knowing nothing but constant construction and everlasting rubble), the sad-sack little sergeant in his baggy, dark green uniform and unpolished down-at-the-heel shoes waved him over to the side. Oglers, gawkers, and idlers dawdled in the enervating midday blaze (like sleepwalkers in a Turkish bath) to see what would happen. By this time the *muttawa* had a reputation for toughness to uphold. Like any street bully, he enjoyed putting on a show. The *muttawa* approached the driver's window. Seizing a hank of the boy's hair and pretending, I thought, more disgust than he felt (the man was an actor), he lifted it disdainfully and asked rhetorically, "Esh *hatha*? [What's this?] Esh *hatha*?" he cried again in his stentorian voice. The boy tried to pull away, protesting that his hair wasn't too long, but the *muttawa* held fast. Everyone in the nearby souk froze their movements in midair, so to speak, watching. The vegetable seller, from Hadramaut in the south, muttered "bastard" under his breath. "You need a haircut," blustered the *muttawa*, "and I'll make sure you get one. Give," he commanded the sergeant, holding his hand behind him like a doctor in an operating room calling for an instrument. The sergeant thrust the shiny scissors into his hand. The *muttawa* pulled the boy's head down by the lock of hair he was gripping, and cut. In a flash of hot shame, the boy burst into tears. "Now go get a haircut," shouted the *muttawa*, flinging the handful of black hair to the ground. The youth, his impotent tears blinding him, desperate to escape the place of humiliation, jerked his vehicle into gear and gunned the motor. Unfortunately, he ran right into a curious lad who was standing on tiptoe directly in front to get a better view. So what had this *muttawa* gained by his last-ditch defense of Islam from the corruption of long hair (ironically, the common and *traditional* style)? Two youngsters had been maimed: one with a crushed pelvis, the other with incalculable hurts unseen.

"He wouldn't have done that to *me*," boasted the taxi driver. "I'd have cut his throat!"

"Don't forget, there was a soldier there."

"What would I care for *him*?" replied the hot-blooded, cologned dandy, giving the loose fingers of his right hand a sudden violent, whiplike snap to indicate what kind of beating he would give the sergeant. Then he opened up as if there were no use in trying to keep the closet door closed when I'd already glimpsed the skeletons inside. He let me know that the generation of old men like that was dying out, and that it was only "a matter of time." Then, in a gentler tone, he added (almost wistfully, as if he were talking about the twilight of some race of doomed gods), "We don't want to kill them, but we do want them to die."

Bob had a map to Dheifallah's "lost village" on the lip of the escarpment; Dheifallah was our ex-student whose wedding we would attend. But he got us there more by "body English" and luck than by Dheifallah's cryptic markings on a piece of notebook paper. The highway we followed was the new Taif-to-Abha road that opened Asir to the world, a route with 117 bridges in its 350 miles. I didn't count the bridges in the two hours we drove before we turned off onto the world's worst road, but there must have been a hundred curving concrete embankments, each one of which bore innumerable scars of combat. Some cars had only had a skirmish, but others had done serious battle and lost: the wrecked bodies, some of them huge trucks, had merely been dragged off to the side to rust. *Khalas!* (Finished!) Every available surface, whether an embankment or exposed stone in a road-cut, had been profusely covered with black spray-can graffiti. You'd think that *some* of that graceful Arabic, especially on the embankments, would spell out the author's exclamatory frustration after a desperate scrape with concrete (*goddammit,* or *son of a bitch*), but they were all either pious ejaculations or Arabia's innocent equivalents of "Kilroy was here." There were no political protests and slogans such as inflame the walls of the rest of the ill-governed world, and crude depictions of genitalia or four-letter obscenities are unknown. Possibly the only roadside scatology in all of Arabia is an official one, and that is a sign on a post near a forlorn cluster of stone houses (most of them abandoned) whose Arabic name transliterates to "Asshair." There it was in bold blue-and-white, and Bob stopped to take a picture of it. A boy herding a few goats on a denuded and rock-ribbed hillside, barren as the bones of a vulture-picked camel, turned to observe us. "That kid probably can't figure out why his village is so famous among the *hawajas.* Can't you just hear the horse-laughs back in that sign factory in Toledo or wherever?"

Here we were in Arabia Felix, all right, a hilly tableland thrust up nearly a mile and a half above the shimmering dunes, thatch huts, and miserable humidity of the Red Sea. Here we were in an Arabia of cultivation and stone houses, of permanence, of husbandry, the fountainhead of the whole Semitic race. And although the sky was as blue as I'd ever seen it, the air as clean as I'd ever sniffed it, still an oppression hovered over me, and I soon realized what it was: I was suffering, and had been since I entered the country, from lack-of-tree anxiety.

This country hadn't always been so bare. Forests existed here once, as they exist today in the Rocky Mountains, and in fact some ambitious ministry has begun a reforestation project. Every few kilometers you see hundreds of little seedlings behind goat-proof fences, awaiting transplant. Forests exist in the Rockies because man has not pullulated there. But imagine eons of teeming overpopulation in the Rockies—trees cut down for fuel, the body of the land stripped bare, goats introduced to take off her very underwear—and in this brown nakedness every valley, cleft, declivity, and fissure filled in carefully to make level terraces where wheat can be grown. The tawny quarter moons of wheat climbing the slopes, the brown crumbling hills, the blue sky and clear air of seven thousand feet—this is old Asir. The rain-catching plots go right to the very top of whatever recessed slope they are filling up, getting smaller as they go, so that the last one will be a patch no bigger than a table, the soil but a fine gravel; but it will be there, that patch, and it will be sown to produce its loaf of bread. Accustomed as I was to the hasty, gray, mortar-and-cinder-block shoddiness of boom-Arabia, all this *work* of human hands, Oriental in its vast patient scale—thousands of little fields, each one supported by a retaining wall composed of millions of rocks, in sheer industry rivaling in eye-sweep the Great Wall—all this desperate husbandry fills the mind with awe. But still I longed for the patient handiwork of nature: some big *trees*. In the very highest places on the escarpment, at ten thousand feet, there are meager stands of juniper and wild olive, mere shrubs of the tree family. But common to the rocky wadis of all the highlands is the acacia, or thorn tree, boughs studded with hard, finger-long sharp thorns, and leaves so tiny and pale green that you have to get close to see them; their limbs cast no shade, but only a "thin sprinkled dimness," as Doughty put it. Nevertheless, it is a sort of tree—it makes an effort at being a tree—

and is better than nothing. Besides, if it wasn't for these great thorny bushes, what would become of all the tissue-thin plastic bags blowing about in the full-bellied wind? Those thorns, and chain link fences, are the bags' only natural enemies, but the fences let go of their prey when the wind changes, whereas a shift of wind over the acacia allows it to snag its victim more securely. Pleasant it is to stand under one of those festooned trees and hear, in lieu of leaves, the susurrous bags, the newly caught ones popping eagerly, the tattered old ones making a dry, plastic rustle.

We turned left off the asphalt and began a four-hour "drive," a torture so exquisite—like being on a bucking bronco—that at last it became exhilarating and hilarious. Bob was disappointed in his desire to be the first "white man" to set foot in Arabia the Old: *hawajas* had brought in high-power lines six months previously and electrified this last dark corner. Even so, the foreigners (Koreans) who plugged Zahran into the modern grid must have at least appeared (with their black hair) nominally *human*, because when a twelve-year-old boy wading in a running gully that we four-wheeled across looked up and beheld Bob—with his red hair, red eyebrows, heat-flushed red face, and red open mouth ho-ho-hoing at some pleasantry of mine—the boy pulled up his dress to his brown knobby knees and hightailed it with the flat-out, birdbrained alacrity of a panicky chicken being chased by a dog.

"White devil come to Zahran." Bob mimicked the peacepipe English of an Indian in a movie Western, and ho-hoed even louder. "That kid thought his time had come. I bet his mother used to threaten him with a red bogeyman when he was bad." (Doughty reports that he was taken for a warlock: "Oh, look, how red he is!" they would exclaim on seeing him.)

It took us four painful hours to cover the forty kilometers from the highway to Dheifallah's village at the kestrel-hovering blue edge of an ancient world. The deeper we churned through the flourlike dust covering the potholed and corrugated "road" into the pockets and wrinkles in those hills that led at last to the eight-thousand-foot drop-off, the farther back in time we went. I could feel in my bones, along with the thoroughly modern shaking up I was getting, the antiquity of it all. It was as old as man, and as we proceeded through the tower-guarded defiles the aspect became ever more open, upland, and smiling: Arabia the Happy, the Beautiful. Twenty-five miles from the asphalt was a time warp or a time hole through which one could see directly— like looking through a pipe—the distant past. Indeed, except for the gasoline engine and the new power line that stalked on supporting stilts across the landscape heedless of local obstacles, this *was* the distant past. We were seeing the thing itself; we were *in* it. There was no other way to get into Arabia Incognita than this, over a road so rough I spent as much time out of my seat as I spent on it. My gold ring was squeezed into a circulation-stopping oval from gripping the bar in front of me to keep myself from being thrown through the canvas roof. There was only forty kilometers left of this kind of road, and it has since been completely paved. But if you wanted to get into Zahran only four years ago, before the Taif-to-Abha road was completed, you had to drive like this the *whole way* (north if from Abha and south from Taif) on unmarked trails blazed by Range-Rovers and Land-Rovers and Land Cruisers which merely followed and made roads of the ancient foot and camel paths. They were bewildering mazes into which people did not venture unless they had come out of them and knew their way back, like salmon from a great river system branching and climbing up ever smaller streams until each one finds the limb, the branch, the fork, and the very *twig* he had left as a fingerling. Dheifallah had done this: come back from the wide world to this tiny village of a few houses, to marry.

We knew we were getting close to the edge of the world when all that remained of the horizon was an ominous lack of it, only a gulf of deep blue space, with neatly terraced patches of wheat marching on tiptoe right up to the edge. When we arrived Dheifallah was standing in his outdoor "bloke" factory, chatting with his two Yemeni workers, waiting for us.

❖

Arabia Incognita

Real estate fever. Dheifallah's house. AWOL in America.
Getting rich. Wedding postponed. Harvest in Zahran. Dheifallah's father. Dheifallah's testiness. Arabs' golden age. Abd
al-Wahhab the fanatic. Emergence of the Saud family. The
Ikhwan. The waterskin. Belief in miracles. The Mecca girl.
Food and eating. Staff of life. A scorpion on my bed. Trying
to sneak a drink. Stumbling around in the dark. Country women
wearing veil to be modern. Marriage a contract. Saudi justice.
Sexual practices. Dheifallah's "homosexuality." The unemployed donkeys. The block factory. "Poverty" in Arabia. Smoking
the hubble-bubble. Yemenis the best workers. An argument.

L ike as not, when you see three Arabs standing around,
even here where the air is Olympian, they will be talking and
dreaming not of Pan and of the sport of gods in the nymph-
fretted forests that existed here of old, but of money. Here in
the remotest corner of Arabia Felix, real estate fever has hit hard,
and speculation in land is rife. Dheifallah took our hands and

walked us the few score yards to the windy ledge overlooking the abyss and showed us where his house would be as soon as he could acquire the piece of rock we were standing on. The house where he lives now, still abuilding on the upper story, he would sell. He pointed to a peninsula shaped like a flatiron that jutted over the dizzy drop-off, and announced proudly (it was corroboration of his own business acumen) that Prince Fahad himself had bought that piece and would soon build a villa on it. Much of this land was soon to be Zahran National Park, Dheifallah exulted (like a developer who had got in at the bottom of the boom), and what he had done, what he was still doing, was buying land he guessed would be in the path of progress, one jump ahead of the government. A financial bulldozer that smoothed everything in its path, it would not be diverted by the inflated price of a hectare here, a hectare there, no more than a tractor blade would haggle with a stump. The trouble for Dheifallah the Speculator was that these farmers who over the centuries had subdivided this ancient land to the inch were not easily bamboozled, so that "this land here," said Dheifallah (we were walking over a patch of wheat stubble no bigger than a house trailer), "costed three hundred thousand riyals." (A hundred thousand dollars! *Zahran National Park!* Was I going to find my pre-Islamic woman *here*?)

Dheifallah now brought us to his new house. He led us into a huge square room, a *majlis* (a male precinct off limits to women except when they came in to clean). It was furnished in the old style: there wasn't a stick of furniture in the room. Along three walls hard bolsters, to lean your elbow on, were placed at intervals of four or five feet on a kind of narrow band of inch-thick foam rubber than ran around the huge room. On the concrete floor was a large blue fiber mat from Taiwan; in a corner by the metal door (with an inch or more of daylight showing under it) five or six foam-rubber mattresses were stacked for guests; and in the two-foot-thick wall on the windward side facing the escarpment was a small unscreened window with wooden shutters inside and black metal bars outside. The plaster walls that rose to meet the cathedral-high ceiling were painted in a color Bob called "Third World green," a shade "somewhere between aqua and vomit." Those huge high-gloss areas of sick color were formidably bare, with only one decoration—Dheifallah's framed diploma from the English Language School where Bob and I had taught—bringing some relief to the eye. Over the diploma was a tube of bright neon, its fixture anchored precariously in the plaster, and from one of the telephone-pole-like beams supporting the upper story there descended a bare weak light bulb on white wire.

In this giant cube Dheifallah ate, slept, entertained guests, conducted business, and, as the eldest son of an aging father, willingly took upon those thin shoulders the responsibility for all his immediate clan. That's the way it is done; a Saudi's commitment to his family is absolute.

We didn't get to meet his bride-to-be or any of the womenfolk of his family, although during the day and a half we spent captive in that room—we were taken out occasionally for exercise—we ate five meals, all of them prepared by the hands of unseen women. They had no idea who we were or why we had come to visit their son, brother, nephew. We could have been plotting with Dheifallah for the takeover of Mecca; they would have been as ignorant of it as the family cat.

To each of the men who came in and out of that room to do business, gossip, drink tea, eat, or to escape being outdoors during prayer time (I saw no religious observances here), Dheifallah introduced us with a slightly defensive air, as if we were some new vice or affectation he had acquired in his travels in heathen lands and was determined not to give up. If he was just a trifle ashamed of their backwardness, they were clearly deferential toward him. Because of his knowledge of the wider world, he had become the de facto sheikh of his clan, a very informal process whereby he who demonstrates ability is followed. The position is not hereditary and is as easily lost as won, and by the same process.

He was the only one of his family to have left Zahran, and he had done it by enlisting in the Royal Saudi Air Force. He was sent to the Dhahran air base for a three-year course consisting of basic training and a smattering of secondary schooling in a Quonset-hut institution long run by the British called TTI, Technical Training Institute. Then eighteen years old, he acquired, under me, six months of intensive English, after which he was sent to Lackland Air Force Base in San Antonio, Texas, for another year's training. When it was time for him to return home, however . . . being in the United States was like being a child in Toyland, and he just couldn't bear to give it all up: his car, his furnished apartment off base with its color TV, his Mexican-American girlfriend. And even though he was not a drinker, just to be able to walk into a well-stocked liquor store was enough (still, after a year) to take his breath away. The freedom! The permissiveness! He went AWOL.

Going AWOL in the more tolerant Saudi system is not the stockade offense that it is in the more Prussian American military; in other words, Dheifallah knew what he could get away with, especially since his family was connected by marriage to the commanding officer of the Dhahran base. He liked San Antonio. So many Saudis were sent there for training that they had an expatriate community going, having parties and celebrating *Eid* (the end-of-Ramadan feast) together. They even bought their sheep from an old Texan who ran a small ranch twenty miles northwest of town. They would kill the sheep in the traditional way: twist the head back so that the neck faced Mecca, pronounce *Bismillah* (in the name of God) over it, saw its throat open, then squat around it smoking cigarettes and chatting while, with nary a bleat, it bled to death cooperatively on the ground. They would then skin it, turning it inside out as you'd remove a wool pullover from an otherwise naked child, leaving the bloody bundle on the ground for the "hawks" (Dheifallah meant buzzards). The farmer, horrified at what looked to him like a heathen practice, eventually forbade any more such sacrifices on his land, though he was still willing to sell his sheep at inflated prices. Thereafter the Saudi students would take the sheep "to a desert place" (a mesquite pasture south of Lackland) and butcher it there. Dheifallah supported himself during this AWOL time on money from home, on funds from his girlfriend, Carmen, and on what he earned from a part-time job parking cars at a downtown garage. The job was a happy compromise. Saudis are very particular to find work that accords with their notions of dignity and propriety. Most Saudis will condescend to keep a shop in the souk, but there are some who consider that only a degrading step above slavery. None will do hard labor; that is work for Yemenis and African blacks. Since taxi driving is a mechanized extension of man's work, cameleering, it is the chosen profession. Thus, in the United States, while Dheifallah would have preferred to starve rather than *wash* cars, *driving* them up and down the ramps was okay.

After a year in America, Dheifallah's homesickness and sense of duty, not parallel lines, finally converged. Somehow he smoothed things over with the RSAF (their manpower is so low that they cannot afford to be too severe with their young men while waiting for them to mature), but the Air Force remained only a nuisance to Dheifallah, not a commitment. Yet he was stuck. Theoretically an enlistment is for five years, but in practice it is for life: in other words, you cannot get out. So Dheifallah had to set about getting rich in boom-Arabia while the getting was good despite the RSAF. This was in the early seventies, and if a Saudi couldn't get rich then it was because he was under twelve, over seventy, or mentally retarded.

The smell of easy money, as intoxicating as spring blossoms, was in the air. It was a mad scramble for money, for housing, for goods. There were shortages everywhere, and yet the foreign companies and their workers who were building Arabia from scratch kept coming in, with nowhere to put them. If you could get a cinder-block "villa" built (as Dheifallah managed to do in Al-Khobar), you could rent it the next day for $40,000 a year. The whole country was slightly mad. The only two deep-sea ports, Jidda on the Red Sea and Dammam on the Gulf, proved inadequate to this buildup, and were overwhelmed. Freighters sat in the water for half a year collecting demurrage while waiting their turn at dockside. "Cement!" cried the builders. "My kingdom for cement!" While freighters loaded with materials were backed up on line halfway up the Red Sea to Suez, another flotilla— hundreds of diesel trucks driven by blond young Englishmen and Scandinavians in shorts—stretched from Europe to the Gulf, bringing in overland everything from razor blades and cigarettes to tractors strapped down on flatbeds.

It was a good thing I hadn't traveled ten thousand miles over land and sea just to attend Dheifallah's wedding, because it was postponed by an act of Allah: late harvest. Nothing takes precedence over a crop to be gathered, otherwise the clan Zahran wouldn't have survived these thousands of years. They survived by working hard in their fields and then defending their produce against the depredations of their more improvident neighbors. Harvesting the crop is what they were doing now in the high clear air above the Red Sea. As I stood on the threshing floor, a large paved circle where wheat is strewn under the plodding feet of the family cow (a zebu that, poor thing, is otherwise confined to a dark and smelly plywood shack), I watched it all: the women in the long layered flounces of yellow, purple, green, and red, gaudy as tropical lizards, welcome bits of color against the dominant tones of brown. Bent from the waist, they move in a line through a field cutting handfuls of wheat stalks with a sickle-shaped knife. Their heads are covered with conical broad-brimmed hats, and they go unveiled except for a sheer muslin scarf (also worn by women in the fields of Andalusia, by the way) to protect the face and neck against chaff and gnats. This stooping and cutting is the women's timeless work; put bronze or flint knives in their strong dark hands instead of the steel, and you could have watched this identical scene millennia ago. But hard on the hennaed heels of the women bearing off the grain, a bright new yellow tractor, driven by a young boy in a white *thobe* and a red-and-white checkered rag piled on his head, turns into the little patch of stubble. He plows it all in a few dusty passes to expose the red soil underneath, then heads jauntily to the next harvested field while an orange-bearded old man, looking biblical, broadcasts seeds over the freshly turned clods from a sack at his waist. They waste no time in this all-important production of food, and when the sun goes down the tractor lights come on and the plowing continues.

The patriarch sowing in the near field turned out to be Dheifallah's father. *Abu* (father of) Dheifallah was a hardy man near

seventy with an orange beard (older men often henna their beards
to disguise declining virility) and the bluff heartiness of a born
politician. When we shook hands he took Bob's freckled wrist
(Bob exudes such good nature that people take to him right away)
and made a comic feint at the bracelet worn there, asking if it
wasn't gold. No, only copper, Bob replied, explaining to Dheifallah—who translated—that it was a souvenir from his war days
in Vietnam. You could tell that this weatherbeaten Moses of the
wheat field was wondering, What war? What's Vietnam? Why
wear a bracelet of copper? But he did understand *war*, and probably thought Bob had taken it from a slain enemy. Judging from
the *khanjar* (curved dagger) worn at his girdle, he looked ready
to deal with an enemy or two himself. In fact he was: he carried
the *khanjar* with him everywhere, Dheifallah explained, his father
beaming and nodding in eager agreement. He carried it for safety,
because "he did not feel good without it." Although he had no
use for it now, in the "old" days they used to "fight with that
village over there." Dheifallah pointed to a cluster of stone houses
only a few hundred yards away, but in this clear air, it seemed
so close that you could see the individual brown flags of stone
against the hard blue of the horizon. Only a few yards directly
overhead, potent and self-contained as a sleeping cat, power lines
hummed. Catching the father's eye, I pointed to the once-hostile
village and then to the wires, and remarked, "Big changes."
"Right! *Big* changes!" Looking idolatrously at the wires, he breathed
a heartfelt *Alhamdulillah* (praise God). With a heartfelt *Alhamdulillah* of my own, I echoed him, but in my heart I went beyond.
I not only praised God for that genie-in-the-wire that pumped
their water out of the ground and gave them light, I praised God
(and the House of Saud) for dragging Arabia, even if with a
Wahhabist rope, into the twentieth century. *Alhamdulillah*, in-

deed. After centuries of dog-eat-dog savagery in "this insecure Semitic world," as Doughty called it, a man can now sow his field without having to wear a knife.

❖

After we left Dheifallah's father (who resumed his biblical sowing) and walked back toward the house, I shook my head and wondered out loud—not very intelligently, I'm afraid, forgetting for the moment that Dheifallah was a Saudi and not another American—where Arabia would be without oil. It was not a tactful or politic question: oil meant foreigners, technology, and Western superiority, and reminded Saudis of their total dependence when, only a few years ago, they were in their infancy. No child likes to be reminded that he is barely out of diapers, no student that a wide gulf of knowledge still separates him from his teacher. But Dheifallah's display of anticolonial testiness—something new in him—far exceeded my breach of tact. He responded with a not-so-idle query of his own. Where would Europe and America be, he wanted to know, if not for Islam and all the Islamic inventions they stole? Uh-oh, what was this? Was Dheifallah a closet nationalist? And why *Islamic* instead of *Arab*? But even textbooks in the West ignorantly perpetuate this mistake, dutifully devoting a chapter to "Islamic" achievements in art, architecture, or whatever. Naturally, Islamic zealots with a religious or racial axe to grind (and holding the view, one hopes, that the sheep-sacrificing part of their religion is an affront to civilized man) have a vested interest in making their dogmas look good. This kind of chauvinism is not confined to them. When I left New York, a new radio program on WQXR called *The World of Jewish Music* had managed to find out which forgotten composers were Jewish, and was playing them with dogged . . . patriotism,

I suppose it must be called. I am of a mind with Doughty, who wrote that their "murderous" religion (I would go further and include *all* religions that divide mankind) should be "trodden out like fire by the humanity of all the world."

Well, I wasn't about to get into one of *those* arguments (my people and their works versus you and yours) with Dheifallah. If he wanted to believe that Islam invented the electric light and the electric chair, too, for that matter, it was okay by me. Besides, I knew what he meant: coincidental with Europe's religion-smothered Dark Ages, the Arabs, fired with a homegrown new faith of their own, were living the good life over in Baghdad, keeping civilization alive—the so-called golden age of the Arabs. Even so, what was done in Baghdad then does not give Dheifallah the right to stand up and take a bow today, no more than a peasant from a Sicilian village could honestly bask in the applause given a Leonardo just because they both happened to share the same language and religion. If the argument is accepted that Islam brought out the best in the Arabs (the license it gave them to go raiding and conquering brought them wealth and civilizing contact with the wider world), then it is equally fair to say that Islam presided over the decline and fall and the long centuries of backwardness ever since. During this time some of the Arabian tribes, on whom the yoke of Islam never sat very firmly anyway, began backsliding into paganism, but were heroically (or tragically, depending on the point of view) diverted from that primrose path through the efforts of a reformist named Mohammed ibn Abd al-Wahhab. Wahhab was a Koran-thumping fundamentalist who would have been as forgotten as any of our radio evangelists had he not shrewdly aligned himself with the local political power, the nascently ambitious family of Saud. Together, this unholy alliance spread out from its home base in Nejd, the oasis-dotted desert around Riyadh, to conquer most of the Arabian peninsula for the first time since the glory days of Islam, and it even presented a danger to Syria and Iraq.

Abd al-Wahhab is always described by biographers as a "sincere" and "inspired" preacher (a fanatic), but like most people who take it upon themselves to reform their neighbors, he and his followers quickly began killing those who resisted being reformed. The Wahhabis and the Saudis (Mohammed ibn Saud was the great-great-great-grandfather of the present king, but when he and Abd al-Wahhab had both passed from the scene, their sons kept the marriage of church and state going) were the Islamic fundamentalists of their day, shunned and abhorred by the more enlightened (lax) Muslims, just as the present-day leaders of Muslim countries (ironically, the Saudis too) despise yet fear the regime-threatening Khomeini and his Islamic diehards. The Wahhabis and the Saudis were so successful, in fact, that the sultan of the Ottoman Empire became alarmed at their growing power and sent two expeditions of Egyptians to crush them. The first one, although it managed to take back Mecca, was defeated when it tried to go farther inland, but the second one laid siege to Dariyah, the Saudi date palm village stronghold a few miles from Riyadh. Following their orders to "leave nothing standing," they cut down all the date trees, leveled all the mud-brick houses, and killed every male. When the Saudi leader, Abdullah, surrendered, he was sent to Constantinople and beheaded. The monster (one half Religion, the other State) was cut in two by this stroke, but no sooner had the Egyptian army marched away—it was the first time, by the way, that a foreign force had penetrated central Arabia—than the two halves were making eyes at each other. They were not, however, able to work effectively together again until a hundred years later, when Abdul

Aziz ibn Saud, father of the present king, changed the course of history. In 1902 he and only a handful of companions retook Riyadh from his enemy the Rasheed, and set about to complete the job his ancestors had been unable to do: unify the tribes of Arabia under Saudi rule. What Ibn Saud (or simply Abdul Aziz, as he is sometimes called) did, after first destroying his local enemies in Nejd, was to settle thousands of Beduin recruits in agricultural and religious communities, arm them for "defense," stir them up against "the unrighteous," and use them deliberately as his fighting arm. These Ikhwan (Brethren), as they called themselves, were true heirs of the zealous Wahhabis. They forbade tobacco and all amusements. Music—even singing and whistling and children's singsong chants—brought reproof. Wilfred Thesiger, in *Arabian Sands*, wrote in 1945:

> He [Philby] told me that once he was sitting with Ibn Saud on the palace roof in Riyadh when they heard someone singing in the distance. Genuinely shocked, the King exclaimed, 'God protect me! Who is that singing?' and sent an attendant to fetch the culprit. The man came back with a Bedu boy who had been driving camels into town. Sternly the King asked the boy if he did not realize that to sing was to succumb to the temptings of the devil, and ordered him to be flogged.

And Doughty has this to say:

> Many Aarab were come to town, and as I went abroad I heard one whistling—a surprising sound in the Arabic countries! where it would be taken for one's whistering to the jinn . . . I never heard a woman sing . . . in these countries. —Where be the Aphrodisiastic modulations of the

fair singing women in these Arabian deserts of 'the Time of Ignorance'? *The hareem sing not in their new Arabian austerity of a masculine religion.*

These modern puritans, these Ikhwan, outdid even their mentors, the original Wahhabis, in the savage ferocity of their warfare. Anyone who opposed them was by definition an enemy of God, deserving death (they took no prisoners), and to be killed oneself while fighting for God assured one instant entry into Paradise, where there was wine and dark-eyed, plump women called *houris*. With the deliberate use of these fanatics who let their beards grow because it was ostentation to trim them, and whose hoarse and blood-chilling war cry as they rushed to the kill was "The winds of Paradise are blowing," Ibn Saud had conquered all of Arabia, from Kuwait to Asir, by 1926. But his troubles were not over. He now had to destroy this monster he had created, because it had turned on him. Had the Brethren purified all of Arabia and raised Abdul Aziz to the head of it, only to watch as he proclaimed himself king and rode in motorcars with foreign infidels? It took Abdul Aziz four more years to bring these arrogant zealots to heel, and much sadness (so it is reported), as he had to cut down his old comrades, but by 1930 it was done. In 1932 he named his austere Wahhabist kingdom Saudi Arabia. A year later another wind was blowing: on a wretched strip of humid desert near a cluster of fishermen's shacks named Dhahran on the Persian Gulf, Standard Oil of California was exploring for oil.

Just outside the door of Dheifallah's big room, in a construction-shaded breezeway area leading to the kitchen, there hung suspended by a plastic rope a black goatskin strutted with water.

"What's that for, Dheifallah?"

"For keep our water cold," he replied with a smile that was half apologetic, half defensive.

"Do you have a refrigerator?"

"Of course we have refrigerator. G.E. But my father don't like. The water is too cold. Besides, he say it is taste better the old way."

It was sufficiently grotesque as it swung there, upside down and fat as a pig, for the photographer in Bob to want a record of it. He paused, aimed, and shot; and Dheifallah was not pleased. He forced a kind of crooked smile, but there was only unhappiness in his voice when he asked, "Why you take picture of that?" Too late, Bob realized that he'd made a typical gringo mistake. To put the best face on it he feigned disingenuousness: "Why not, Dheifallah?"

"We have everything here in Zahran to take picture of: fields, tractor, power lines, new house—but you take picture of *that*. Then when you show it later to your friends," he added, "they all laugh and think we are Beduin."

"Dheifallah, that's not true. I *plan* to take pictures of everything—I've got five rolls of film—but we just got here and the light is perfect right now." But Bob had a point, too, brought out when we talked about it later: "*Fuck* those Third World sensibilities. If Dheifallah was ashamed of that fucking goatskin, why didn't he hide it? I *saw* it, didn't I? Did I ever tell you about my trip to India? How mad a policeman got when I took a picture of a mile-long line of men all taking a shit along a railroad track? If they're sensitive about foreigners taking pictures of their nasty habits, then why the fuck don't they do something about the way they live? They could dig latrines and cover them with canvas. They're just too fucking lazy."

We went into the big room and sat down (leaving our flip-flops by the door) while Dheifallah went into the kitchen to call for tea. Saudis have to drink their weak sugary tea every two or three hours, like a drug. I had pulled out my notebook to record the conversation above, and was writing in it when Dheifallah reentered, gave me a sharp look, kicked off his sandals, and brought the tray to the center of the room. "First we will drink tea together, then we'll eat." We gathered around the tray, sitting cross-legged on the floor. He poured the tea, and lifting his little glass mug and smiling, welcomed us, his "first teachers," to "the Kingdom of Zahran."

"Thanks. And look, Dheifallah"—I hastened to apologize— "I hope I didn't offend you with my remark about oil."

"Well, it's because when I was in States nobody know about Saudi Arabia and think we are all Beduins riding camels. But you see that's not true. We in Zahran are here when Americans are killing Indians and living in log houses."

"But your father said you were fighting that other village only a few *years* ago."

"Didn't the cowboys fight each other? Before there was strong government? And they had big open country, too. Here, we are lots of people in small place. Somebody take one inch of other man's land, there's big fight over it."

While we sipped our tea Dheifallah told us how some villagers were fighting once over one of those inches of land, and had reached the point of bloodshed, when at night a giant snake slid over the land, measuring it with his mark perfectly to everyone's satisfaction.

"What kind of snake was it?"

"Very big snake."

"I mean, what's the name of it? You have those kinds of snakes around here?"

"No. Special snake. Allah send it."

"Oh."

Another such dispute was settled, Dheifallah claimed with a straight face, when a fence dividing the land appeared overnight.

"What do you mean, 'appeared'? You mean somebody built it?"

"No, impossible for people. *God* do it."

"Oh."

Doughty wrote:

Commonly the longer one lives in a fabulous time or country, the weaker will become his judgement. Certainly I have heard fables worthy of the Arabs from the lips of excellent Europeans too long remaining in the East. How often in my dwelling in that hostile world have I felt desolate, even in a right endeavor: the testimony of all men's (half-rational) understanding making against my lonely reason; and must I not seem to them, in holding another opinion, to be a perverse and unreasonable person? . . . their world is to thy soul as another planet of nature. Their religious wizards converse with the jan, the cabalistic discovery of hid things is every day confirmed by many faithful witnesses.

Truly, a goat's palate is more discriminating than the Arabians' reason. Tales of flying snakes guarding buried gold, of instant cures, of jinn—all these things, where there are no skeptical intelligences at work, are believed by all Arabians from the king down to the local Beduin. The more improbable and magical the hearsay, the better. Dheifallah's story of the Mecca girl is an instance.

A teen-age girl, after accompanying her parents on a year's sojourn to the States, was hard to manage when she got back to Arabia. She primped all day, she listened to rock and roll on the shortwave, she cut her hair, she painted her long fingernails, she wore high-heeled shoes, she spoke rudely to her mother, and she pouted and was unhappy. (She had caught the American teenage sickness, all right.) Then this unhappy "girl catch disease," Dheifallah said (it was probably an exotic germ brought in by an outlandish hajji from some "shithole," as Bob would call it), and died. She was buried outside of Mecca in a shallow grave, sort of like the kind you'd scratch out in the backyard for a favorite cat or canary, except that the family pet would probably have some little stone or stick set up to mark the spot. Not so the Mecca girl in Wahhabite Arabia, where any show of veneration for the dead is idolatrous. According to Doughty,

> The corpse is washed, and decently lapped in a new calico cloth: they scrape out painfully, with a stick and their hands, in the hard-burned soil, a shallow grave . . . and over the pitiful form of earth they heap a few stones . . . yet I have seen their graves in the desert mined by foul hyenas, and the winding-sheets lay half above ground.

A few days later a boy following some goats through the burial ground, lunar in its waste and desolation, heard a noise that sounded like crying coming out of the earth. Naturally he did not stop to investigate, but ran for his life. It was the Mecca girl, of course, come back from the dead. Well, as if this survival-in-the-grave wasn't preposterous enough to choke a horse, the credulous Muslims swallowed hard and got down to the real juice of the story. When they dug her up, they found her lips and her cheeks rouged (they had washed the body and trimmed the nails before she was buried), but—Dheifallah dropped his voice—her fingernails had grown two inches and were *red*. This was shocking enough, but it was her *feet*—Dheifallah's voice dropped down to

127

a whisper—that caused the townspeople and the ulema to gasp in horror: the bones of her heels had grown long and pointed, exactly like those *high-heeled shoes* she was so fond of wearing. "Al-*lah*," I said. And did Dheifallah believe this? "*Wallah*," he assured me; it was seen by many people—it was the talk of Arabia. And where, I wanted to know, is this unfortunate girl now? Oh, she's dead. God only let her live long enough for her to apologize to her father (her *father,* mind you), and to be a warning to other Muslim girls by her example.

The most interesting thing we did in Zahran was eat. We ate like Zahranis because Dheifallah liked his mother to cook the old-fashioned food for him when he came home, dishes no longer available in the modernized Arabia outside these western mountains.

The staff of Zahran life is bread. Dheifallah's shy, almost sullen younger half brother, Ahmed, who pulled up in a big Mercedes truck in time to eat with us—and left the rackety motor running right outside the window, so that our first taste and aroma of the authentic old diet was flavored with diesel smoke—spurned the thick wheaten rounds for some white-flour flaps he had picked up in Bahha on his way in from Taif. When our dinner was ready, Dheifallah spread a square of oilcloth on the floor, then in two trips between our room and the kitchen (which, with its women, we were never to see), he brought the food. No utensils of any kind, no glasses: a large enameled bowl of cool soured milk was held in both hands as it was passed around, a gift of that gentle-eyed zebu ungratefully confined in her manure-spattered plywood shack. Then we hove up on our haunches close to the communal dishes and began to eat. In this matter, too, as in so many other human activities, the Arabians are artless. Get the thing done and never mind the details—that is their way, whether it is throwing up a cinder-block house or eating. No sitting on lawn chairs in the predinner calm of evening looking out over the darkening Red Sea rift toward Africa, cocktails in our hands or mellow platitudes in our mouths in hardheaded Zahran. Life had been—until yesterday, almost—too nasty, brutish, and short for there to have been time to cultivate any human possibilities other than survival. Many generations of such behavior, obviously, are not forgotten in only one.

Once the novelty wears off, eating with just your right hand is about as much fun as making mud pies with the kids in the backyard, and as messy. Fortunately we had the hot bread to use as a sop and even, once Dheifallah showed us how, as a spoon. You took a little ball of the moist bread and made an impression in it with your thumb, then you dipped that into the bowl of *samn* (clarified butter) and the meat broth, and hoped it didn't spring a leak on its way to your mouth. Same way with the okra, cooked with tomatoes to a delicious pulp—scooped on a crust of bread and brought precariously mouthward. It was almost worth coming to Zahran just to eat that bread. Made of the wheat growing all around us, about the size and shape of a nearly deflated soccer ball, the color of a rhinoceros in a dust wallow, it was baked in a charcoal oven and was God's gift to the Asiris and Zahranis. Seeing us devouring it with such relish, Dheifallah urged it on us, which he didn't have to do. I asked Ahmed, who kept his skullcap on his head but had his *ghutra* draped over his shoulder (they are forever fiddling with these bothersome head-rags, which a modern Arab needs like a drugstore cowboy needs a Stetson, but they cling to them with the same kind of perversity with which they avoid using spoons), why he preferred that white bread when the other was available. He only replied that he "didn't like" it. I think I know why; since nobody in his right mind could prefer the taste or texture of white-flour bread over the Zahran loaf, I suspect he regarded the one as old-fashioned and the other as modern. I understood. It was years after I left Texas before I would cook—much less admit to myself that I liked—pinto beans, corn bread, or turnip greens. But Ahmed didn't get his perfect teeth and athlete's body from a childhood diet of white bread. And the way he got his broad shoulders, his muscled arms, and his callused hands was by fighting the wheel of that Mercedes truck all day over bad roads. Ahmed was not loquacious; something was eating him. Besides, he had a young wife inside whom he was eager to see. With a pointed remark to Dheifallah that, unlike some lucky people, *he* had to get up early and hit the road, he rose, went out to shut off the motor, and was not seen again until the next evening.

A shadow passed across Dheifallah's face, but he was immediately the sunny host again, joking that since I was so fond of their bread, I should become a Muslim, find a wife, and settle down in Zahran to live to a ripe old age. To encourage me, he held up as an example a great uncle of his who married a new wife at eighty, fathered two children, and lived to be a hundred and thirty! I had heard time and again from my students about the almost biblical longevity enjoyed by many of the people in these mountains, but I doubted some of the most extravagant claims (125 years upward) because no records were kept (or are today). But after this allowance was made, why wouldn't the Asiris and Zahranis have been a long-lived people? They grew their wheat in those terraces up and down every mountainside, they ground it, and they ate it. The air is pure; there is not a factory or source of pollution within a thousand miles. So why wouldn't a person with a strong constitution live a century as a matter of course? Who knew? Wasn't it possible that the composition of that vertical upthrust of sedimentary rock that formed the escarpment, which crumbled down over the eons to form red soil, contained "longevity minerals" that less fortunate people didn't get?

Close to bedtime, as we started pulling foam mattresses off the stack in the corner (I was hoping that Dheifallah would disappear so I could take a swig from a bottle of sidiki I had secreted in my suitcase), we uncovered a black scorpion, said to be less dangerous than the sand-colored ones. Surprised, it turned in a cautious exploratory half circle, its tail arched. Dheifallah picked up one of his discarded sandals by the door and hit it, but on the yielding foam rubber he did not kill it. He had to hit it twice again before it lay broken and quivering in a leak of its own fluid. The trouble was the opening under the door, which, in the dark, even that "special snake" that "God send" could crawl through, and I hoped even more fervently that Nature would call Dheifallah out into the night, and soon, so that I could dull my dread of creeping things with a slug of rotgut. What *I* would have liked to do, being a practical American, was turn everything over in the room. There were only the bolsters and mattresses; and then, satisfied that the scorpions were outside where they belonged, I would have stuffed rags under the door to make sure they stayed out there. But talk about fatalism! Dheifallah didn't even investigate the three remaining mattresses! He didn't go outside, either, for yet another cousin (there had been three so far) popped in—without knocking, of course. There is no such thing as privacy, nor is there any desire for privacy. The way they see it, anybody who locks his door to keep people out is probably up to something either sinful or illegal (most probably both, where church and state are one). On the other hand, the kind of loneliness that many of us in the West have learned to endure as a kind of by-product of our way of life is unknown among Arabians. This cousin, a foppish beanpole who wore his *ghutra* and *egal* pushed so far down over his eyes that he could hardly see out, who followed the fashion by wearing his sandals way too small for his feet so that his heels touched the ground as he shuffled along, advised Dheifallah to *eat* the *agrab* (scorpion) in order to gain immunity from its sting. He explained that you toasted it over a fire in a shallow coffee roaster until it was nothing but a powder; this powder you stirred in water and drank. So much for Arabian folk medicine, I was thinking, when Dheifallah came up with a remedy that a witch doctor would have envied. He stated, as casually as you'd prescribe an aspirin, that if you drank a tea-glassful of gasoline right after a scorpion sting, you would not feel any ill effects. Well, I knew what *I* wanted to drink (although some Americans in the kingdom feel that sidiki is not much better than gasoline and refuse to drink it), and the arrival of yet another guest gave me a chance. This was a short, ugly man in a gray *thobe* whose tongue had all the desperate energy of a wild horse trying to shake a rider. It was soon joined by Dheifallah's, no slouch in disputation either, and a loud argument broke out. I half expected it to end in blows as their voices rose and fell in passionate duet. It was about money, of course, with much accusing and denying, and many *wallahs* and *wallahis* on both sides. It was hard to follow, but it had to do with a load of sand Dheifallah had borrowed from the ugly man, and some blocks (they pronounced it "blokes") put on consignment. No way to settle it, apparently, but to go to the "bloke" factory right away, talk to the Yemeni workers, and look at the papers they had signed. (Saudis are aggressively litigious; every other one is involved in a lawsuit.) They left.

No two conspirators, their moment at hand, ever looked at each other with as much significance as did Bob and I just then. I snatched the bottle of "brown" (whiskey-flavored sidiki) out of my suitcase, handed it to Bob, then stood by the door, not to hold it shut, of course, but to engage whoever came in long enough to give Bob a chance to tuck the bottle away behind a bolster. But nobody came. We tilted our nightcaps in uneasy but undisturbed peace. I was not, however, able to settle down now in the welcome glow of alcohol and write up my notes in the dim green room. "Goddamnit," I said.

"What?"

"I've got to go out."

Just outside the door stood two plastic pitchers of water and a little box of Tide that Dheifallah had pointed out to us earlier: "There's water if you need it." What you were supposed to do was take one of the containers with you, squat, pour water into your left hand and wash. Then, on your return, you would scrub that unclean hand with the Tide. So much for easy theory. I was gone ten minutes. When I returned, I had chaff in my hair, my clothes were disheveled, and I was bleeding from a scratch on my ankle. If it seems that I make too much of this going-out-of-doors, that I exaggerate the difficulty of it, especially since previous travelers were obviously able to take such small miseries in their stride and didn't find them worth mentioning, well, I would like to invite you to put yourself in my shoes. Close the door of the *majlis* behind you, as I did, and stand there in the black night facing this unpleasant task. Across the valley a tractor was plowing with its lights on, but that didn't help me. A neon strip above the door lit the area immediately around, and served as a beacon to guide you back, but a few feet away you are confronted, in the absence of a moon, with total blackness. I did not take the water; I carried a length of yellow toilet paper in my shirt pocket. The Zahranis, of course, know their land in the dark as I know the rooms in my house; but it was steep, rough, tilted, terraced, unfamiliar, and irregular, and if you walked too far in the wrong direction, you'd fall a mile into the Red Sea. There was the "road," and the Mercedes truck, which I felt my way around with the help of some light coming through the room's one small window, but I wanted to get a little farther away. I didn't want to leave a little flag of yellow paper right in the road for the morrow's light, and that's when I found beneath my feet a steep slope and loose rock that carried me in a kind of sliding roll down to a patch of level ground. I could feel the sharp wheat-stubble. Deciding this place was as good as any, and hoping there wasn't a scorpion under me, I did the best I could under the circumstances and even found, reaching around with my hands, a stone to place on top of the paper to hide it. There is no doubt that the use of water makes a neater job of this business, and I was glad that the Zahranis had not learned to change their ways. Can you imagine anything more unsightly than yellow, pink, and white wads of toilet paper scattered from Zahran to Asir?

Dheifallah came back a little later, but Bob and I, pleasantly (if illegally) crocked, had already gone to bed and I was half asleep. I would have been fully asleep were it not for a gang of mosquitoes that had been resting up and fasting all day and were now wide awake. I covered myself with the sheet, but they poked through it where my face and hands touched. Bob and Dheifallah were similarly covered; we looked like three stiffs in the morgue. I felt like shouting in the dawn light (often in Arabia it was all I could do to keep from throwing up my hands): "Why the hell don't you cover that window with a screen!" But we seldom do what we ought to do. I heard Ahmed come out, start the truck, and roar off to begin another long day on the road; and I reflected how unfair was our common opinion that Arabs are lazy. Which Arabs? In Asir and Zahran I had seen only heroic husbandry and industry. If the *desert* Beduins were "lazy," it was because they knew only famine, thirst, and hardship, and even a colony of yodeling Germans, transplanted in that desperate land, couldn't do any better. Nobody works harder than Mexicans, and yet when I was growing up in Texas we perceived them in the same way. It takes no Freud to figure out why, just as it takes no Goebbels to appreciate the value of a propaganda so effective that before I ever laid eyes on an Arab, I despised them. It helps, when you take someone's land, to picture the owner as undeserving of it anyway.

I went outside in the sweet first light to piss and splash some water on my face. If, last night, my problem was grope-darkness, now, ironically, I found the light awkward. For I was not alone—all Zahran was astir at this hour—and I was not dressed right, either. An Arab, squatting inside his white dress, is a common sight that excites not a second look, but an American in trousers, both vertical and horizontal against the horizon at the same time, could not be missed. While I stood there wondering where to go, a young woman, unveiled, wearing a dress of such bright yellow that it seemed to make her black hair even blacker, came out of the breezeway area behind the goatskin to scatter some food scraps to three or four skinny chickens. She was as surprised to see me as I was her. "*Sabaah al hayr* [Morning the light]," I said automatically, but she only averted her face and hurried back inside. Obviously, *she* wasn't that hospitable widow I had hoped to get a glimpse of. In fact, if this scared-rabbit behavior was representative of Zahrani women, they aren't as free as the Beduins Doughty lived among a hundred years ago. The *hareem* (wives) were always chaffing him, concerned about his single life, urging him to marry. He was often left alone with them, and at least one good-looking widow asked him to marry her. When the Saudi kings, to justify to the ulema their introductions of electronic gadgetry, used the argument that it would more effectively propagate throughout the kingdom the "Islamic way of life," foreigners (who expected the opposite) winked and nudged each other; but this is exactly what *has* happened. Purely local or tribal customs that thrived in ignorance of the outside world and even of orthodox Islam are disappearing in favor of one *national* conformity. As an example of one of these tribal customs, Burckhardt (*Travels in Arabia*, 1829) writes that when the puritan Wahhabis discovered to what length the Merekede tribe carried hospitality (the host giving the guest his *wife*), they forbade it. When no rain fell for two years, the Merekede begged permission to be allowed to honor their guests in the way practiced for centuries by their forefathers. Of course, the Wahhabis knew that Allah sent the rain (if it pleased Him) in response to prayer, not fornication, so it is very unlikely that they would have allowed this shame out of the Age of Ignorance to continue. However, it was about this time that their movement was crushed by the Ottoman Turks, who had become alarmed at the Wahhabis' growing power. So it is possible that the Merekede, with the Wahhabis gone, reinstated the practice, only to have it stamped out for good a hundred years later by the resurgence and triumph of Islamic fundamentalism in our time. Anyway, as a result of this national conformity, young women in the villages, knowing that their city sisters go veiled, don the horrid thing because they want to be modern. It's enough to make you break down and cry.

You'd think that a man who had lived in the States for two years, and among Americans in Dhahran for six, would have left off for a while the brown man's burden—guarding his females—and introduced us to them. There were four or five women over there in the kitchen. I know, because three of them, wearing conical

straw hats and carrying sickles, went out into the bright morning
to cut wheat, yet when Dheifallah, at eight o'clock, finally rolled
out of his shroud and went to order tea and breakfast—beans,
eggs scrambled with tomato, and more of that bread, the better
for being left over—it appeared forthwith.

Over breakfast, again on the floor and without utensils, I asked
Dheifallah if he was disappointed at the delay of the wedding.
He said simply, "No." They do not marry for love. If, as is said,
the idea of romantic love, chivalry, and dalliance was introduced
by the Arabs to the crude peasants of medieval Europe, whose
style of lovemaking, according to Shakespeare, was like that of
a "full-acorned boar (a German one) who cried 'O!' and mounted,"
it is we who now carry the idea of woman as pure sex object to
them. The idea of love does not enter into a Saudi marriage. It
is an arranged contract. Because these contracts are not made in
heaven but in Riyadh, members of the armed forces are no longer
allowed to marry foreign women. Too many young men, sent to
the States for training, were in the habit of bringing back a blond
"play-pretty." Having a blue-eyed American wife was wonderfully
modern and classy, but with the honeymoon over, it inevitably
led to tension between the American embassy in Jidda, which
knew what the woman was up against (I know of one American
woman who was smuggled out of the country), and the Saudi
government, which said she couldn't leave without her husband's
permission. And that wasn't the only problem: the Saudi girls
who should have been these boys' brides were being left high and
dry.

I asked Dheifallah how much he had to pay for his wife. It
was a bald question, I admit, but it was a bald fact, too. Poor
Dheifallah. A less worldly Saudi would have simply quoted a
figure, and then innocently asked what wives cost in America
(as between two hapless men caught in a similar bind). But

Dheifallah, feeling an obligation as a budding nationalist to justify some of the more embarrassing aspects of Saudi life, tried to downplay the mercenary cast of the agreement by reminding us that the money paid to the girl's father is used to buy clothes and gold for the daughter, and furnishings for the house. These items, he pointed out rather impatiently, make up her trousseau and are hers to keep in case of a divorce. That was true, but there was no law requiring the father to spend all of that money on the bride, and in fact most fathers didn't. In addition to these expenses, the bridegroom has to bear the cost of the wedding, which can range from expensive to ruinous. The success of a wedding depends on the number of sheep killed. The more guests you invite, and the more sheep you kill to feed them, the bigger the man you are seen to be. How big a man was Dheifallah? About a twenty-sheep bridegroom. At $150 apiece, that would add another $3,000 to the $15,000 he had to pay his bride's father as hostage against a hasty divorce. While it is true that a man has only to pronounce "I divorce you" three times to get rid of his wife, it is not nearly as easy as it sounds. First of all, as a safeguard against a rash or angry pronouncement, a man may not merely blurt, "I divorce you I divorce you I divorce you, you bitch!" at one breath. He must go before the local judge on three different cooled-off intervals. Even so, the pressure on a man *not* to divorce—to smooth out his differences with his wife—is tremendous. There are family and tribal interests inhibiting the merely capricious decision made in pursuit of personal happiness, and as further insurance against rashness, there is that large sum of money that the husband forfeits. But if he does go through with it, the divorced wife goes back into the care of her father or brothers. No blame attaches to her, and she can marry again, though with loss of virginity her price falls. Anyway, with another thousand or two for incidental expenses, it would cost Dheifallah

$20,000, or two thirds of his year's Air Force salary (a salary doubled by a nervous royal family after the attempted coup and shoot-out in Mecca in 1979), to get married.

"At those prices," I teased, "do you think you'll ever be able to marry your quota of wives?"

"Now, you see? This is what *all* Americans think—that all Arabs ride on camels and have four wives."

"No, Dheifallah, Americans know that all Saudis ride in Cadillacs, wear sunglasses day and night, and have four wives *at a time*: divorce one batch, take on another. Anyway, what's wrong with having four wives? A lot of Americans envy you. There've been times when I wished I had four wives."

"Now he doesn't even have one," offered Bob, rattling the conversational cage.

Briefly, because he had met my wife in Dhahran, I told Dheifallah of my divorce. He was amazed when I told him something of American divorce settlements.

"You've heard of women's liberation, haven't you, Dheifallah?" chimed in Bob, smiling wickedly.

"That's crazy. I think what you need is man's liberation."

"Listen, America is a good country to be a woman in these days."

"Or criminal. You put killer in jail awhile, then let him out. When I was in States, man called Son of Sam was killing girls in New York. They catch him, they put him in jail, maybe they let him out already. Why?"

"I don't know. Well, I do know—but it's a complicated problem."

"What's complicated? Man kills somebody, you kill him. *Khalas!*"

"You don't have to convince *me*," said Bob. "I agree with you one hundred percent."

I have seldom met an American in Arabia who did not approve

and admire their swift, harsh, and *human* justice. It's human because it's direct, it's one-on-one, and it's satisfying. It also presents a man with a deep moral dilemma: he has a choice, he acts, and he lives with his choice. As an example of an unsatisfying and *in*human way of justice, take the American way, as illustrated by the following story, which I proceeded to tell Dheifallah and Bob. The wife of a man of my acquaintance was rollerskating to the liquor store to buy a bottle of wine for dinner one evening when a man from a drug rehabilitation halfway house attacked her and, before he could be stopped, beat her to death with one of her skates. The husband was ready to do the human thing, strangle with his bare hands the animal who had killed his wife, but he never got the chance. The murderer was whisked away by the police and processed through the System: courts, psychiatrists, counselors, state-appointed lawyers, what have you, while my friend vainly tried to keep track of his whereabouts, hoping to catch him somewhere alone for five minutes. But he never got that chance, and eventually the System swallowed the killer up completely; the husband lost track of him. He did locate the man's mother, to ask *her* if not her son the unanswerable question *why*, but the mother, half crazed herself by a life of junk food, TV, bad air, and white-trashdom, only told him what he already knew: that her son was a bad egg, that she was not surprised that in a moment of rage he had murdered a stranger on the street.

Before this appalling tragedy, my friend had never given crime or punishment much thought, except to hold very vague enlightened ideas: if asked, he would say he was against the death penalty. But after he saw his wife a bloody mess on the sidewalk, he knew where he stood. Oh, he was for the death penalty, all right, and he wanted to be the one to deal it out. The matter, however, was taken out of his hands (where, as the party who had suffered the second-greatest wrong, he felt it rightly belonged) and put into the hopper of the penal system, where it would go around and around for years. It was at about this time, when my friend's hot thirst for vengeance had cooled a little, that I told him what a Saudi, in a similar situation—except that Saudis are not crazy and do not kill on the street—would have been able to do.

There would have been four choices available to him. First, he could have killed the man himself. "Stop right there! That's what I would have done!" cried my friend. "Well," I said, "wait'll you hear them all. Second, if you were too squeamish to do the job yourself but still wanted him killed, the government would do it for you. Third, since killing the man wouldn't bring your wife back, you could accept a large payment of what is called 'blood money' from the man's tribe." "A *curse* on his low-life tribe! What's the fourth choice?" I took a deep breath before I answered. "You could let him go . . . 'into God's hands,' as they say."

Now it was my friend's turn to take a deep breath, and pause a long while. Finally he said, "Yes, I see the beauty of it. Well, what would *you* do?"

"I don't know," I said.

"What do you mean, you don't know?" demanded Dheifallah. "That's one of the big troubles for you Americans. You don't know what you believe. Are you say that you not kill this man if you the husband?"

"Like I said, I don't know."

"Well, I know what *I* do."

"Yes, because your society is a lot simpler, you have far fewer people—only five million in the whole country—and you have a clear belief."

"We have Koran, we follow it, we are sure."

"You don't have any doubts about it?"

"Why we have doubt? It tell us all we need to know. *We* know what to do with man who kill woman with rolling skate."

"All right, but that's a clear-cut case. Most Americans would know what to do, too, if they had the chance. But take something that's not so easy, like adultery. *You* know what to do. You put the adulterers to death—even though the Koran doesn't say that— but we don't think adultery is that serious."

"Koran doesn't say what?"

"That an adulteress should be put to death."

"Yes, it say that. Stone her."

"No, it doesn't, Dheifallah. I just read it again a month ago." (What I could stand of it. Most of it is taken up with retelling the Bible stories, but they come back weirdly skewed. It is only in the last suras from the Medina period, which address the problems of women, marriage, food, laws, etc., that it gets interesting.) "There's a *hadeeth* that Mohammed allowed his followers to stone a woman for adultery, but I don't believe it. Mohammed was always saying that God was compassionate, merciful, forgiving, and I believe Mohammed was, too. Do you know when stoning women for adultery started? Have you heard of Abd al-Wahhab?"

"Yes," he said, looking worried that I might ask him more, and pouring us out some more tea.

"Under him. And not everybody went along with it then, either. In fact most of what you do comes not from the Koran but from *hadeeth*—what so-and-so told so-and-so, who told so-and-so, who wrote it down, what Mohammed was supposed to have said or done. Take this business of shaving your armpits. Why do you do that?"

"Mohammed do it."

"You show me where it says that in the Koran. Your bride is

shaving her pubic hair to get ready for marriage, right? Well, where does it say so in the Koran?"

"*Wait* a minute." Bob's attention, beginning to flag under all this religious talk, picked up again. "*I* didn't know that. Why do they do that, Dheifallah?"

"More hygiene," Dheifallah replied, not very happy with Bob's keen interest in this subject.

"Maybe it's more hygienic," Bob chuckled, "but less alluring. I'd guess cunnilingus is not very widespread." Dheifallah did not understand what "alluring" or the other word meant, and when Bob told him he blushed. "Don't you go down on your women, Dheifallah?" asked Bob.

"No way."

"Or the other way around?"

"If woman try do that to me, I lose respect for her."

"That's interesting," said Bob. "With me it's the opposite."

"This is for whore to do. Not wife."

"What is the wife for?"

"For fucking."

"Well, we consider *all* that as 'fucking.' What do you consider fucking?"

"In the way of Islam."

"What way is that?"

"When man gets on wife, he must say *Bismillah* [in the name of God]."

"Is *that* right? Pardon my asking these silly questions, Dheifallah, but this is all new to me. And does the wife say that, too?"

"No."

"Well, what should she do?"

"Nothing. Only she must get up and wash, and man, too. My girlfriend in San Antonio was dirty like this. She never want to

Dale Walker

get up, never want *me* to get out of bed after fucking, but just lay there. Once she want me to fuck her when she have period."

"Did you?"

"No way. *Harram* [Forbidden]. Blood make men sick."

"No, it doesn't, Dheifallah."

They are such hypocrites, but like children without self-knowledge, they are unaware of it and therefore untroubled in conscience. When Dheifallah condemns this and that as *harram*, has he forgotten, I wonder, his homosexual days in Dhahran? That too is *harram*, forbidden by the Koran, but conscience sits lightly on the Saudi: he does whatever he can get away with. Neither have they any notion of justice for others. A man will rise from his homosexual bed to gawk at the stoning of an adulteress, without being troubled by the obvious unfairness. Quick to feel a wrong directed against him, he is not as hot to put himself in another's shoes and feel that injury as his own. It's every man for himself—better him than me! When I told my students how Jesus one day prevented the execution of a woman charged with adultery by telling the self-righteous Jews, "Let him among you who is without sin cast the first stone," they murmured and fell silent as their light-skipping souls, like feet encountering quicksand, were slowed and held by these immortal words. When I asked them how it was that I knew their Koran well enough to dispute with them and yet they knew nothing of the Christian Bible, which is not allowed in the kingdom, they saw nothing strange in that, since Islam was the true religion!

Dheifallah's homosexual companion was Musa, a big-faced English-language retread (he had been put through the cycle twice and still failed to get a passing grade) with glittering eyes and a habit of slowly licking his lips when he caught Dheifallah's eye. Free himself for the day at one o'clock, he would appear

144

regularly in our office looking for Dheifallah at that hour of after-lunch stupor when young men's thoughts often become libidinous. Hand in hand (many men hold hands when they walk together, but never a man and woman; her place is a couple of paces behind him), they'd go to Dheifallah's room in the barracks and lock the door, a thing so ordinary among the young men that it excited no comment. As long as Dheifallah remained the "man"—Musa was delighted to play any part, he told me once—he acquiesced in this arrangement with a manly grace. As for the rest, that could all be fixed with Allah later, in roughly the same manner that the AWOL was straightened out with the Dhahran base commander.

We got so tired from sitting around all morning, discussing pubic hair and other weighty matters, that after a lunch of *kepsa* (chicken with rice), we took a nap. In the quiet heat of the day I could faintly hear the women's tireless voices next door. A dry breeze (and some flies) blew in through the window. Gentle, irregular, slightly asthmatic snores from Bob. Nearby, the beastly braying of a donkey, a noise especially keyed to disturb men's guilty noon slumbers. I raised myself on an elbow to look out the window. Judging by his lazy tumescence, the donkey was venting his male frustration at a cruel god who fashioned him for heroic bouts of insemination (the only remaining purpose of his sunstruck days), only to have his capacity—like a painter with plenty of paint but no canvas to work on—thwarted by the indifference of female estrus. There he stood, semi-erect in the midday heat, bewildered by it all, braying to the depths of his poor male heart, with tongue so protruded it looked as if he were trying to spit it out.

I lay down again. Far off, the soft popping of a gasoline engine water pump—a kind of pressure on the atmospheric tympanum like a rapid throb in the temples—was the only anachronistic sound in the timeless village drowse of midday. That pump is what put the donkey out of work. Unemployed and unprized, the donkeys roam free. We saw them all along the roads in Asir and Zahran, because the roads followed wadis where there were standing pools of water and vegetation. Apparently their only enemy was the Mercedes truck; the bloated bodies or bleached skeletons of recent and old kills littered the shoulders of the asphalt. I could never figure out how the Arabians arrived at their notions of "lawful" meat. They eat the *dthub* (monitor lizard) and the camel and the locust, but not the donkey!

The camel has been retired now as well, by the machine that roared up at sundown with a load of sand for the "bloke" factory, an open piece of ground not far away, to which Dheifallah walked us. It was an operation of primitive simplicity that entrepreneurs in countries of more advanced capitalism could only envy. It was an innocent capitalist Garden before the Fall, before Sin brought about government displeasure. No such interference from Riyadh, however; it stood aside and let the Arabians do what they did best—buy and sell. Arabia is one gigantic freewheeling souk. Dheifallah's "factory" was a pile of coarse sand, some bags of cement, and a made-in-Germany iron form that passively produced two "blokes" at a time: placed on the ground, it was simply lifted off the stiff cement mixture that was shoveled into it. The new blocks were watered twice a day for a couple of days to keep them from drying too fast and crumbling, after which they were stacked up until sold. The two workers who made the blocks were Yemenis—both of them short, dark men in knee-length dirty skirts and worn-thin rubber flip-flops. At this hour of westering sun they had removed their red-and-white checkered head-rags and wore them slung over a shoulder. Finishing the day, one of them watered down the blocks and the other, at a word from Dheifallah, set about stoking the *shisha* (water pipe) for us to smoke. There was nothing for us to do but sit cross-legged on a fiber mat on the littered ground (mostly Velveeta cheese cans) and watch them.

Arabia is the only "poor" country that does not make one feel guilt at one's own good fortune. While there is no hunger, living conditions are often as wretched as anywhere in that Poverty Zone that stretches from Central America to India. But you will not find that beggarly resentment, that sense of permanent and sullen inferiority such as you see elsewhere. No, the Arabian, never enslaved, meets you eye to eye with frank equality or even, yes, a conviction of his own innate superiority. Thus, while it was Dheifallah who indicated a desire to smoke the *shisha,* it was the Yemeni day laborer—not a servant but a host—who took charge.

On one flame of his two-burner gas-bottle stove, he boiled water in a black kettle for tea. On the other, in a Maxwell House coffee can with holes punched in it, he fired a few lumps of palm charcoal until the edges whitened. With charcoal-smudged fingers, he dipped into a sticky tin and took out a handful of gunk called *jerock,* a fermented fruit concoction imported from Pakistan with the sickly sweet smell of rotten apples, pears, and mangoes. This moist black mixture he put into the ceramic head, which was about the shape and size of a large artichoke with the top half cut off. He pushed it firmly down onto the shaft of the *shisha* (so that it looked like a decapitated artichoke on a stem), placed a ceramic wafer over the *jerock,* and filled the rest of the head with charcoal. He then picked up the *shisha*—with its five brass filagreed legs, it was as tall as he was—and set it near us, with its hose, sewn up in a gaudy decorative sleeve of rags, coiled on a hook supported by the shaft. That done, he placed in our midst on the ground a much-dented aluminum tray with a full pot of tea and three little glasses.

When the dry escarpment breeze had blown the charcoal white, Dheifallah put the wooden mouthpiece of the hose to his lips (indrawn so that no saliva touched it) and sucked in a deep breath, drawing air through the water gurgling in the bulge at the bottom of the shaft. Dheifallah exhaled slowly (no smoke yet, but this preliminary drawing down of the hot air over the *jerock* was necessary to get it burning), put the mouthpiece back to his lips, repeated this dragging and exhaling several more times to the deep agitated gurgle of the water. Then, bending back the mouthpiece and holding it clasped against the hose, he passed it to me. It is considered offensive ("like handing somebody a limp dick," another Saudi explained to me once) to offer the hose straight on. My turn now. I drag deeply, doing my part to get the *jerock* hot enough to start burning, and when I am quite dizzy from hyperventilation (after a few breaths you get light-headed and swear you're smoking something other than rotten fruit), I pass the hose to Bob. He makes the water gurgle mightily, and finally—on his shift, so to speak—his exhalations begin to come out light blue: the stuff has begun to burn, the smoke gets denser, the sweet smell of it permeates the sudden calm of sunset, and now we can pass the hose, take moderate drags, and enjoy this delicious water-cooled smoke.

There is a folk belief in the West that the Arabs smoke hashish (an Arabic word that means simply "grass," by the way) in these pipes, but that is not true. In the first place, possession of marijuana or hashish is a very serious offense in Arabia the Strict, much more severely punished than alcohol use (fifteen years for first offenders, *death* for stubborn cases). Second, one would not want to waste it in such a way, almost the equivalent of throwing it into a bonfire. No, the only high produced by this smoke comes from an unwonted excess of Allah's own oxygen. But because it helps the Arabian, for a dreamy lapse, to escape from his miserable land and climate, his austere customs and prayers—and may even start up a song in his heart—you can see why the Wahhabis could detect in this self-absorbed smoking the hand of the devil.

As we sat on the ground, sipping tea, gurgling the *shisha*, and engaging in the pleasant pastime of watching others work, Dheifallah assured us that Yemenis are the best workers. Next in desirability come Indians, after which are Pakistanis and Egyptians. He will not hire Egyptians except when nobody else is available. I asked why; were they lazy? No, they were not exactly lazy . . . he wasn't sure what it was; he just didn't like them. But, I prodded, wouldn't their Arabic-speaking make them preferable to the Indians and Pakistanis? Dheifallah replied that they spoke Arabic badly anyway, and then he mimicked their speech. I was reminded of an Anglophobic American making fun of the Brits. The only *good* thing about the Egyptians, he declared, was that the Saudi who hired them—out of a polyglot throng of day laborers at the "work souk" in Taif, a place that used to be the old slave market—was allowed to keep their passports, so they could not escape. This passport-keeping policy has led to abuses, as some unscrupulous bosses, trying to reduce their labor costs to nothing, were in the habit of keeping some ignorant, just-off-the-plane Indians and Pakistanis in a state of virtual slavery. This lack of control, he said, was the Yemenis' only drawback; while they spoke down-home Arabic, did not put on airs like the Egyptians, were more productive and intelligent than the Pakistanis, and earned their top wage of a hundred riyals a day, they kept their passports and could "run away" whenever they wished. In fact, he sighed (if that tea had been a pitcher of mint juleps and that bare ground a veranda, we could have been three southern gentlemen discussing our niggers), it was hard to keep a Yemeni more than three or four months at a stretch. When they got homesick, they only had to board a Jimps, pay a few riyals, and in three or four hours they were in their mountain homes. Then, when the Yemeni had chewed his fill of *ghat* (a mildly narcotic plant whose young green leaves Yemenis chew dreamily all after-noon while Yemen—a country not traveling anywhere at a great speed anyway—comes to a halt), caught up on the local gossip, fathered another child, perhaps, and felt himself ready for another stint of work, he had only to cross the border and show up any morning at the Taif slave market. Being a Yemeni was like being a Mexican wetback without the Border Patrol.

Dheifallah's two Yemenis cost him nothing to keep. If Arabians are anything, they are independent: fatalistic, cheerful, patient, they expect little from life, and are not disappointed. Take that house of theirs a few yards away: four walls about five feet high enclosing fifty or sixty square feet of ground. It may have taken them an hour to stack up those loose cinder blocks. Planks were laid across the top, scraps of tin and plywood put over those, and, to keep the wind from blowing them off, a few old tires and rocks. The lintel above the doorway was a piece of two-by-four to which a red rag was tacked, and that was all. It was the kind of thing that boys on a summer day would put up and call a "clubhouse," better than a palace. I mean it as a compliment to the Arabians, to their lack of materialistic attachment to things, that they sort of "play house" all their lives. It is the kind of house that you see at every factory and housing project and construction site in Arabia, thousands of them scattered through-out rubble-Arabia, and in places like Jidda, where it hardly ever rains, they dispense with even that and simply live outdoors. But whatever the case, you never pass by and think to yourself, "Oh, my, these people are *poor,*" because poverty, mostly a state of mind conditioned by the welfare state, is not known here.

❖

We were up early to the strains of a quarrel (background music, it seemed, to the modernization and financial exploitation of Zahran) between Dheifallah and his half brother Ahmed. I learned what was eating Ahmed, and that was mankind's commonest complaint: he felt overworked and undervalued. The trouble in part was that new Mercedes truck, Ahmed's pride and joy. He had wanted it, coveted it, lusted after it, and now he was married to it. It had cost 170,000 riyals (about $50,000), was paid for in cash, picked up at the Jidda dock, and driven carefully home. Just as the Arabian, slapdash in other matters, always took good care of his camels, so it was with Ahmed and his truck. He kept it clean and greased, and he changed the oil and filter frequently. In boom-Arabia, the possession of this machine was a guarantee of prosperity: there probably wasn't a family in Asir and Zahran that didn't have a son out on the hot roads, hauling and dumping. With the Mercedes, Ahmed can make 15,000 riyals a month, which means that the family can pay off its investment in a year. (Arabians have an eye for quality; although there are cheaper American and Japanese competitors on the market, Mercedes's reputation for durability under the harsh conditions of Arabia is proven.)

But while Ahmed with his callused palms was constantly shifting gears and fighting the wheel over bad roads and steep grades, he had time to brood over his condition, which, in its darkest moments, seemed to him to be a kind of indentured servitude to that truck. He knew he was doing *his* share, but when he got home from a hard day's hauling and saw his brother, cool as that goatskin in the breezeway, drinking tea and smoking the *shisha* with his two infidel friends, he wasn't sure Dheifallah was doing his. Of course Dheifallah had a just argument of his own: several persons could ride in a car, he pointed out, but only one could steer. Dheifallah, because of his education, experience, and wider contacts, had to mastermind the whole shebang.

Finally diplomacy, and Dheifallah's unassailable position as head-of-family, ruled the day. Ahmed, mollified, climbed into the cab, slammed the solid German door, ground the gears (along with his teeth, probably), and drove off. Somehow (the Protestant in me coming out, I suppose), *I* felt guilty for contributing to Dheifallah's delinquency, and so, having seen what was left of old Arabia, I was content to remove myself before my host wished me gone.

PART THREE

ARABIA
AMERICA

❖

Taif

Farewell to Bob at Bahha. Killing chickens and scaling fish. Chance meeting with a "Saudi-Texan." Women being hauled in a pickup. Othman the smuggler. Description of smuggler's country. How I met Othman. Thirsty princes at my door. Othman gets rich breaking the law. A friend fixed up with a "Saudi princess." Hailstone-chilled sidiki. Women available if you can afford them. A nap on the sidewalk. Corruption in the royal family. A public telephone call. The king passes. The "showplace of the Middle East." Pilgrims stop for the night. Ashtar and paganism. The holy Black Stone of Mecca. What it looks like.

Bob offered to drive me (he even pretended he wanted to) all the way up to Taif, my next logical stop. Taif was the nearest large town, and I had friends there where I could take a desperately needed bath. But I pretended, just as convincingly, that I *enjoyed* being dirty, and unshaved, and itchy; and besides, I pointed out, how was I ever to catch a glimpse of Arabia's elusive equivalent of the Himalayan snow leopard (the Hospitable Widow) if I didn't take every opportunity to put myself in the way of her?

"Widow-schmidow," scoffed Bob. We were driving out of Zahran on that same axle-straining "road" that we had come in on. "There ain't no such animal," he concluded. "Good old Islam has conquered everywhere, like bad money driving out the good." Then, looking at me carefully, he observed, "Even if you found one, she'd have to be a blind nymphomaniac with a bad cold to stand *you.*"

Bahha, the widest spot in the road between Abha and Taif, was the market town of the Ghamdis, in *bilad* Ghamid. A thousand feet lower in altitude than Zahran, and farther from the escarpment, its long main street—a mile of highway running through an arroyo—had the dry, chalky look of the American Southwest. We were like two prospectors come to town. After four hours in Bob's Land Cruiser, white as a flour bin from the dust we'd churned up, our reward (to bring Thesiger up to date) was not a drink of "pure, nearly tasteless" water (we had Pepsis), but a smooth asphalt highway. Truly, our relief on getting onto it was immense, and so sensuous as to be sinful. The heavenly peace that descended on us passed mortal understanding. In the shade of the *gahhwa* the blissful spell continued as we blinked mindlessly out at the white midday glare like two lizards baking on a rock. But by and by the cold sweet drink gave us a pickup; we stirred our road-sore rear ends and limped out to the Land Cruiser. Since I'd be seeing Bob soon, there was no need for a good-bye.

"See you back in civilization," said Bob.

"I'll pick you up at Kennedy and bring you home for lunch. What would you like?"

"Need you ask? A case of beer and two fat pork chops!"

There I stood, still ragless in the hot swoon of midday, on the litter-strewn shoulder of the highway. The *gahhwa* was connected to a gas station, which had spread a stain of petroleum (along with empty cans of oil, blown-out tires, and oil-sodden cardboard boxes) twice its own area, as if the grease-soaked sand had acted as a blotter. There is nothing that depresses my mind with more weary horror than a gas station in Arabia at hot noonday. It is even worse than a cinder-block mosque with a loudspeaker mounted on it, and the only thing worse than *that* is a Southern Baptist church at eleven o'clock on a hot Sunday morning when they're singing the doxology. God, just *look* at it: that baked highway, reeking of petroleum and diesel smoke; slender men in white dresses sleepwalking through the thick heat, which slowed them down as if they were wading through molasses. Over there, the dumpy figure of a woman, all in black, crossing the road and unable to see well enough through that black gauze to judge the speed of a Mercedes truck bearing down on her. A blast of an airhorn hurried her along. *Why* is she wearing that awful thing? Are these people *sane*, making a woman go shrouded like that in a heat-absorbing garment out of which she can hardly see?

Well, I wasn't getting anywhere just standing there criticizing them, and, as God's spy, I wasn't doing my job, either. *His* job was to judge, mine only to report, but I confess I often got the roles mixed. Taking my suitcase in one hand and my shopping bag in the other (I left that rug I stole with Bob, to be shipped home free with his own household goods), I started walking through the town strung out along the highway toward the more central part of one-story cinder-block buildings, trash, and smashed cans.

In the main part of the souk, under an airless tin shed, the chicken seller was doing a lively business: he'd open the cage

door, reach into the white squawking melee, and drag out by the
foot or wing a leghorn who with gaping beak pierced the bright
midday air with his sharp-tongued cries. However, either because
the proprietor was trying to fob off a sick or skinny bird, or because
he was suspected of it, that one was immediately rejected by the
customer in favor of another he pointed out in the cage. When
the customer was satisfied that he'd gotten a good one, he'd hold
it upside down by the wing or leg (one man had a streak of ordure
down the front of his white *thobe*) until the helper took it from
him. Meanwhile, the blood-spattered Egyptian helper was busy
killing the chickens. Throwing the chicken onto a bloody marble
slab, bending its head back (rather like the mouthpiece of the
shisha that Dheifallah handed me) so that its neck faced Mecca,
he pronounced the obligatory "*Bismillah*" (in the name of God)
in a bored, ritualistic grunt, "*illah*" being the only audible part,
and sliced its neck with a butcher knife. (It is important that
chickens be killed *Bismillah,* or "kosher," as it were, so important
that overseas processing plants that kill and freeze chickens for
Saudi consumption have been provided with a tape recording
that intones the necessary word over the production-line slaugh-
ter. Otherwise, you see, the orthodox Muslim . . . oh, well, never
mind.) The Egyptian then thrust the chicken headfirst into a tin
funnel set up over an old oil barrel to let it bleed and kick at
heaven with its yellow claws. When all that was left of life was
an involuntary shudder or two within the cone, a spasmodic
clutch of claw above, the Egyptian grabbed the corpse by the
feet and dipped it into a big pot of dirty water kept on the boil
by a burner attached by a rubber hose to a gas bottle. Then he
switched on the automatic plucker, a cylinder to which were
fixed dozens of soft rubber knobs. As the cylinder revolved at
high speed, the Egyptian held the chicken by the feet and turned
it this way and that against the knobs until all the bedraggled

feathers were knocked off against a piece of filthy tin that served as backstop. It was then eviscerated, dropped into a plastic bag, and handed to the customer.

At the next open-air booth the fresh-fish seller, whose merchandise comes on ice from Jidda, takes the fish the customer selects out front, places it on a scaly board, and chops at it with a dull hatchet until its fins are off and its belly is open. He strews the guts on the fly-crazed sand. His scaler is a plank into which a score of tacks have been nailed, the points protruding from the other side. With this he scratches at the fish, the flying scales sticking to his hair, his eyebrows, his arms, and his bare feet. He then dips the fish into a pail of bloody water, slides it into a clean plastic bag, and *khalas!* it's done.

A blue and white Silverado slowed and stopped. "Where you headed, pardner?" Those words came out of the mouth of a Saudi of about my age behind the wheel, but the accent was pure Texas.

"Othman!"

"I *thought* that was you."

"Well, it is."

"So you came back."

It is taken for granted that nobody leaves the Magic Kingdom for good. Consequently, when a face drops out for a few years and then reappears, there is little surprise.

"Not exactly. I'm here on a visit, on business."

"Selling, huh?" (Another assumption that would normally be accurate is that "old hands" never die; they come back as sales reps.) "You going to Taif? Hop in. Throw your suitcase in the back with all that junk." His pure Texas speech and his pure Saudi looks were so incongruous that it was hard—even though I knew him—not to laugh out in delighted surprise.

The junk that filled the Silverado looked like the makings of a national Beduin museum. Most of his "junk" had to do with coffee: dozens of that quintessential Beduin relic, the *della* (a brass or copper beak-spouted coffeepot), blackened on many a bed of coals; brass mortars and pestles; and long-handled iron coffee bean roasters and stirrers. In the idle Beduin life, the day was divided between napping and roasting, pounding, and sipping *gahhwa*.

"Allah!" squawked the loudspeaker on the cinder-block mosque. "*Moham-med ra-sool Al-lah!* [Mohammed is the prophet of God]," it crooned, a reassuring lullaby over the cradle of somnambulism. From near and far, the rattle and bang of storefronts closing down as this Friday morning ended. If there were any miscreants awaiting punishment or execution, now would be the time for them to tremble, because Friday after the midday service is the time of reckoning. "Let's get out of here," said the Saudi-Texan. "You ready?"

I was always ready to put distance between myself and all such misleading institutions as religion, but when I pushed aside a box of Beduin jewelry on the front seat to make room for my shopping bag and pulled the door shut, I said disingenuously, "Look, it's prayer time. If you want to pray, I don't mind waiting."

"I take it you haven't become a Moslem?"

"No."

"Well, it's like a friend of mine said, 'It's those who have the least who pray the most,' and he wasn't only talkin' about the things you own, he was talkin' about what you have upstairs."

Othman was one of the persons I had planned to look up, to see how he was faring. We had been friends in Taif, but he was such a hail-fellow-well-met character—like a traveling salesman—that he had "friends" everywhere. I always took pleasure in being with him. Every American in Arabia who does not, like a shocked snail, withdraw immediately into the compound's shell and stay there for the duration of his contract, finds himself longing to meet a worldly Saudi, one sufficiently outside the culture to be able to interpret and make comprehensible the formidable *foreignness* of the place. Othman had done this for me in the past and was to do so again only a few minutes later as we gained on a white Datsun pickup. In the bed of it were huddled two women, their black garments whipping in the wind. With a hand that poked out of the black sack with which she was covered, each held it and the veil together at the throat. As we passed them, the sleek black gauzy ovals that were their faces turned to follow, and I saw in the cab a bearded man driving, and a teen-age boy beside the other window. It was such a common sight that I nearly failed to notice it. That's the danger of a traveler being too familiar with his subject—he loses his virginal eye.

"Don't say it," warned Othman with a smile.

"Don't say what?"

"That those women are being hauled around like sheep."

"I didn't say it," I said with a grin, but he had read my mind.

"Because, you know, it *looks* worse than it is."

"Well, I hope so. Because it couldn't look much worse, unless they tied ropes around their necks and let them run along behind."

"I know how you see it. But look at it the way they do. They are Beduins. They don't think they look like sheep. They don't feel like sheep. That truck is just like a camel. Driving it is man's business. Besides, it's cooler in the back than up front near the motor."

Fair enough! He was right, and I was guilty of that worst crime of the Traveler, jumping to conclusions.

Othman was a heartening example of the human spirit surviving against the moralist's inhuman dreams for the Betterment of Mankind. He was not interested in articulating a philosophy,

161

but if he could, it would be that of an extreme laissez-faire, "that government governs best which governs least." Never mind that the government tried to make men moral: imagine how grim life could be in the United States if some insane sect of religious fundamentalists got the power of the state behind them. No, Othman was a realist who saw men as they were. The Wahhabis could prohibit alcohol till doomsday, but Othman knew that men liked to drink, wanted to drink, and *would* drink, even if this happiness were pursued at the risk of life and liberty. When, therefore, alcohol was banned for non-Muslims by the king in 1951 (following the tragic shooting of the British consul by one of the king's own drunk sons), the smuggling and bootlegging that had been going on anyway for the thirsty Muslims only intensified. It was big money. Othman got his start as a smuggler, and the way he did it in those early days (late fifties and early sixties) was to load up a big Mercedes truck in Jordan and drive into Arabia across the unmarked and unpatrolled desert, avoiding the border stations and checkpoints, coming onto the highway well inside the country. Then, only an innocent lorry among many others (so, with heart in mouth, he hoped), he would drive on to Riyadh, park late at night outside his sponsoring prince's villa, unload the hundreds of cases of Scotch with the help of a couple of servants (recently freed slaves who had elected to stay on), and drive off in possession of the empty truck, his reward. If, however, he got caught in this capital crime, he was strictly on his own. The prince didn't want to know him. Altogether, Othman had made a dozen such runs, but after the second one he had paid more heed to his own safety and kept ready, just under the tarp, a motorcycle on which he could get away in case anything went wrong and he was in danger of being caught. On a motorcycle, on that hard-packed desert, he could outrun anything, and could get out of sand if he did run into it. He sold each truck that he received, and after the twelfth one he built a villa of his own in Taif. Thereafter he retired from active smuggling and became partners with his Riyadh-based prince, receiving shipments of whiskey at his own ornamental iron gate: he became the Taif distributor. So long as he remained in the service of his prince, he secured immunity from the law.

"It's all who you know," said Othman the Realist. While he was waxing fat and rich smuggling whiskey under royal protection, ordinary wretches who didn't know anybody were being caned at hot noon in filthy public squares for the crime of being caught drinking it. You might say they were being punished for being stupid. Othman was not stupid; his success under a repressive system came from not being stupid. But, repressive as the system undeniably is, it should *not* be understood that Saudi Arabia is anything like a police state. As Golda Meir once sweetly remarked, "If the Arabs ever learned to queue up, they'd be dangerous." Well, thank God, they have not yet learned to do so, not even enough to protect themselves from those who have. It is, despite itself, a good government, and were it not for the Arab's fatal penchant for bureaucratic paper-shuffling and *wasah*, that deep-rooted Arabian vice of which the late King Faisal despaired (*wasah*, also called vitamin W, means palm-greasing, influence-peddling, and nepotism), it would be ideal. While it lets the bright and the energetic get ahead, it does not neglect the stupid or the lazy or the unfortunate. Hospitals and schools are free, a student with a yen for higher education need only apply, and interest-free money to build a house, with a thirty-year payback, is available to anyone. The government, however, does not believe it should kill enterprise and initiative by pensioning off the population; instead, it deliberately takes every opportunity to be generous and to circulate the wealth through the economy. Everybody has an uncle or a brother who was given five or ten million riyals (they round it off, like Monopoly money) for some little cinder-block hovel or for a patch of desert real estate that stood in the path of Progress.

Speaking of progress, since one man's enemy is another man's friend, so Othman, while he would certainly be beheaded as public enemy number one by the Wahhabis for his crimes, was, for that very reason, a hero to me. We met as lawbreakers, appropriately enough, drinking Scotch at a mixed party of Saudis and Americans gathered at Othman's to celebrate the footfall of the first earthling on the moon. The incredible event was generously (if insincerely) referred to as mankind's achievement, though it was perfectly clear to everyone, as we listened to the event on shortwave, that it was a marvelous triumph of America's technology. The Americans were justifiably proud of their clever countrymen who could shoot three men to the moon and back, and the Saudis who were present, though they would have liked one of their own along, still managed to get a vicarious patriotic charge from it all, since they had gone to school in America and retained a fund of goodwill toward their second country and language. The *ordinary* Saudis, of course, didn't believe that it was happening at all: the religious ones on the premise that Allah would never permit it, the ignorant on the obvious grounds that it was impossible. These people still ran to the mosque during a lunar eclipse to pray to Allah to take the shadow away. Anyway, glasses of Scotch in our hands, Othman and I began talking; and when he discovered that I made my own beer, we wound up leaving the party to sample it. There's Neil Armstrong on the moon, I thought, and here I am in Arabia, a similar desolation, drinking yeasty homebrew.

Othman, in his enthusiastic and authentic Texas twang (the man had a perfect ear), pronounced it "better'n Lone Star," which shows more what deprivation can do to one's judgment than to the quality of my beer. Actually, compared to the nasty homebrew encountered occasionally in the unsanitary habitat of some foreign bachelor, mine *was* superior. While cans of concentrated Blue Ribbon malt were available then, before the ministry in charge of imports caught on to its real uses, it alone, with water and sugar, did less to satisfy one's thirst for beer than increase the longing for the real thing. But I was able to mail-order from the States a lighter, Pilsen malt to mix with the heavier Blue Ribbon, along with loose, dried hops that I added to give my beer a clean, faintly bitter aftertaste.

Othman considered me his discovery, boasting to his princely friends and government pals, "Hey, I know this guy up in Taif. . . ." He would sometimes, when he was in Jidda, make the three-hour drive up the mountain with a couple of his friends to sample my beer. I never disappointed him or them, and in fact I was flattered to have gotten such an instant entree into high society. When I opened my apartment door (in that building where the goats wandered up and down the stairs) and saw three or four high-placed Saudis on the landing, stately, grave, and well groomed, like a delegation of oil honchos at an OPEC meeting, in this humble place to see *me*, well. . . . Later, when we had loosened up some, I thought, "So this is royalty." Of course, the royal stuff in the Saud family has been diluted and spread so thin (there are thousands of princes and princesses, all of them on the dole) that a close whiff of it hardly takes your breath away, such as contact with the more heady flowers of European royalty might. If it were not for a barely noticeable deference always paid to these young princes by their friends, in fact, I would not have been able to distinguish them from the ordinary Saudi.

But they were the royalty, as royal as you were going to get where everybody in the country, including the Saud family, were Beduins at the turn of the century; and Othman, as courtier, put me in mind of one of those urbane Jews of medieval Europe who, inheritors of a long civilized tradition, acted as friend and adviser to the unwashed, upstart Throne. The similarity went even deeper, for Othman belonged to a kind of outcast tribe, the Sleyb, or Solubby. In a couple of pages devoted to this curious people, Doughty records, as one theory put forth for their situation, that they lost all their animals to stronger neighbors in the eternal *ghrazzus* (raiding warfare), and thus declined, turning resolutely from the vicissitudes of herding to the surer, albeit poorer, gypsy trades of tinker, blacksmith, and hunter. Like the Jews, adversity had sharpened their wits, and in this dire land, where only the fit survive, the Solubby made it. Something of this gift for survival must have animated Othman. Without a strong tribe behind him to catch him if he fell (as a sort of "orphan," as he called himself), he gravitated as a boy to Aramco in Dhahran. In those days, that's where the action and the power were, and he hung around like a stray cat until he was taken in by somebody and made a teaboy. His parrotlike ability in the new language (Texan), plus his ingratiating personality, got him in time a place as live-in houseboy for a Texas family. When that family "rotated stateside," they took Othman with them. After some special tutoring, he was able in one year to learn what American children absorb in eight, and then he went to high school in Houston. The experience, he said, "fucked me up royally," because "I didn't know what I was," but eventually he realized he didn't have to be one or the other, he could be a "Saudi-American."

Back in Dhahran with Aramco (not as teaboy now, but as "public relations coordinator"), he found he didn't like the nine-to-five routine at all: "In that respect I am definitely *not* American." He was at heart a Beduin, raised in a society where the audacious, the brave, or the ruthless could acquire wealth at one lucky stroke while the plodders were only likely to have what they had so patiently accumulated taken away in one violent moment. This was the time-honored way, and if any Saudi needed a reminder, he needn't look any farther than the example set by the father of his country, Abdul Aziz ibn Saud. Actually, look is all he has to do, for the official version of the story is aired on the state-run TV every six months or so, replete with sound effects, Egyptian extras, dramatic music, and a narrator. The purpose is obvious: to found a dynasty, and to create a mythology for it. The moral, however, is so clearly a case of the murderer enjoying the spoils that you'd think they'd stop showing it. But no, they not only keep alive the fact that they owe their fortune to a murder by their founding father (he killed a rival chieftain in Riyadh in 1902), they keep reminding other would-be leaders how easy it was!

Othman was not ruthless, but he was audacious and brave, willing a dozen times to risk all on the desert behind the wheel of whiskey-laden trucks. On those booze-buying trips to Jordan and Lebanon, incidentally, there was another kind of contraband to be had, so, on the theory that he might as well be hanged for a goat as a sheep, he took to carrying back in a foil bag something that looked like a lump of earwax and had a resinous smell— prime Lebanon hashish. He would bestow on his prince half this treasure and keep half for himself, not to sell but to give away, for he knew that in a society that still placed a lot of value on liberality, to be esteemed generous was the highest praise. Listen to what Wilfred Thesiger, in *Arabian Sands*, had to say about this:

Two days later an old man came into our camp. He was limping, and even by Bedu standards he looked poor. He wore a torn loincloth, thin and gray with age, and carried an ancient rifle. . . . The Rashid pressed forward to greet

167

him: "Welcome, Bakhit. Long life to you, uncle. Wel-come—welcome a hundred times." I wondered at the warmth of their greetings. The old man lowered himself upon the rug they had spread for him, and ate the dates they set before him, while they hurried to blow up the fire and to make coffee. He had rheumy eyes, a long nose, and a thatch of gray hair. The skin sagged in folds over the cavity of his stomach. I thought, "He looks a proper old beggar. I bet he asks for something." Later in the evening he did and I gave him five riyals, but by then I had changed my opinion. Bin Kabina said to me: "He is of the Bait Imani and famous." I asked, "What for?" and he answered, "His generosity." I said, "I should not have thought he owned anything to be generous with," and bin Kabina said, "He hasn't now. He hasn't got a single camel. He hasn't even got a wife. His son, a fine boy, was killed two years ago by the Dahm. Once he was one of the richest men in the tribe, now he has nothing except a few goats." I asked: "What happened to his camels? Did raiders take them, or did they die of disease?" and bin Kabina answered, "No. His generosity ruined him. No one ever came to his tents but he killed a camel to feed them. By God, he is generous!" I could hear the envy in his voice.

In time, therefore, Othman became the man to see when the Saudi, dulled by work and prayer, wanted something else out of life ("Beer? I know this guy up in Taif . . ."). Like a true poli-tician, he was always careful to have little outstanding loans out everywhere—in the form of favors, of course—that he was in no hurry to collect.

Whiskey and dope! These were serious crimes, stumbling blocks for the Muslim at the gates of Paradise, wherein for eternity there was wine and those dark-eyed, plump women. If, however, the Saudi couldn't wait until Allah called him, or if he suspected it was all a hoax, and this miserable desert was all there was, here again it was Othman who could come up with something—the ultimate sin—for the here and now. This was The One, all right; and what raised it from the rank of private peccadillo and made it such a delicious indulgence was the capital nature of the punishment.

Was he, then, pimp as well as bootlegger and dope smuggler? Sort of; only not for money. What Othman was after was respectability, position, and influence, and the only way for him to get them was by doing favors for others. Memorable favors, so that when, for example, a contract was to be given out, and a "finder's fee" was to be collected, Othman's friends helped by pushing the contractor he was backing. Although, in absolute terms, the fee didn't amount to a hill of beans compared to the huge bribes of millions of dollars paid routinely to princes by American defense contractors, one little contract for Othman could result in hundreds of thousands of riyals in cash, not bad for a poor boy. These days Othman did not do any more matchmaking. And despite his car full of souvenir junk for the foreigners, he did not actively keep shop in the souk anymore; a cousin kept that part of the family business going. Othman was now well set up: rich and respectable. We can forget those early days; when a pump is flowing strongly of its own, the fact that it once needed priming to get it started is forgotten. He traveled now on buying trips for his own amusement and as a cure for midlife restlessness. The truth is, he took to the road because he was at heart a Beduin. Visiting the tribes on the back roads of Arabia in his beat-up Silverado, sitting with them in their tents or in a town *gahhwa*, it was as if he were still following his grandfather's trade as tinker, still retained the Beduin's age-old hunger for "the news," and savored the telling and the hearing. He knew everybody between Abha and Dhahran, from the Beduin in that black tent yonder to the king.

I never availed myself of Othman's good offices, but I knew an American who did. Tony was an Italian-American who had only two fingers of forehead under a curly mop of hair, who wore a gold chain on a hairy chest, and favored thin shoes and tight pants without pockets. He was headed for a career in the Navy until he found that he could make a lot more money, and have a lot more fun, as a civilian with defense-related contracts wherever the American military wasted the taxpayers' money abroad. He had been all over Southeast Asia when the Vietnam War was in full swing, and his life was an exciting round of money, booze, and women. He was one of those men who claimed to be unable to live without the frequent solace of a woman's body, even if those female attentions ended with disconcerting abruptness, like a parking meter, when the time ran out. His ambition (a harmless one, compared to many) was to "have" a woman from every country he lived in or visited, until he had "had" a woman from every country in the world. Now here he was in Saudi Arabia, in a culture so grim and forbidding and dangerous (Hey! They *stone* people here!) that he didn't know where to start. Tony had no doubt that his hair, chest, tight pants, and natty shoes would, if given a chance, prove irresistible attractions in an open sexual market. But how could he bring those strengths to bear in a mysterious and sinister place such as this, where the women were so many unapproachable black sacks on the street? On his consoling R & R's to the neighboring fleshpots, he steeped himself in female flesh, and added to his growing (and impressive) list of countries where he had "had" a woman, but his contract was nearly up in Arabia the Bleak, and he was as far from a close encounter with a female native of the place as the day he got here.

Then he met Othman, and the mysteries of the East were revealed to him. Yielding to importuning, Othman told Tony to be in his shop at a certain time on a certain day so that a princess, behind the anonymous security of her veil, could have a look at him. This was the chance that Tony had been waiting for. Accordingly, on the appointed day, dolled up like a Mafia chauffeur, and twirling his car keys nonchalantly on a finger, he and his heady miasma of eau de cologne walked into the shop, where Othman and a black sack were deep into dusty bolts of cloth.

"Othman! Hey-hey, *paisan!*" Tony tried to sound casually exuberant, as if he'd just dropped in to say hello. The veiled face turned in his direction. Tony put out a hand with a gold ring on its pinky to Othman, flashed a smile at the princess, and had no idea what to do next. Even acknowledging the princess with a smile might have been a mistake; the proper (and safe) way to react to a Saudi woman was not to react to her at all, as if she wasn't there. Othman came to the rescue: "Just walk around a little so she can see if she likes you, then leave." Tony, whose back was to the princess, gave Othman an alarmed roll of his eyes, but Othman said, "Don't worry, she doesn't speak English." So, humming a tune and lashing his car keys against his thigh with the masterful impatience of an officer with a swagger stick, Tony, keeping the better side of his profile to her, moved here and there pretending to examine different bolts of cloth. After he had done his best to strut and pose without seeming to, he again stuck out his hand to Othman, shouted with manly exuberance, "Okay, *paisan*, be seeing you," glanced at the princess, sighed, and left.

Tony couldn't sleep, wondering if he'd made a good impression on the princess, but . . . relief! The next day Othman assured him that he had. Now Tony, who shared a portacamp with a roommate on the company compound, needed a place to bring her. There was one decent hotel in Taif in those days (1969), but it would never do for a foreigner to even be seen on the street with a veiled woman, much less check into a hotel with her; the executioner would be there with his sword in five minutes.

It was arranged that Othman and the sack (it could have been his wife, mother, sister, cousin, daughter) would walk on a certain street at a certain time when Tony pulled up in his car and offered them a ride. Looked innocent enough: American friend, etc. Othman got in front, naturally, deposited the black sack on the rear seat, and (this is where I came in) they proceeded to my apartment, which I had just rented against the imminent arrival of my wife.

There was no need for greetings or introductions, and there were none. Tony and the sack disappeared down the hallway and into a bedroom while thunderheads that had been billowing in golden glory over the escarpment all afternoon let loose in a gust of cool, grit-laden wind and big spattering drops of rain. Wooden shutters banged shut throughout the apartment building (so new that it still smelled of wet plaster) as the breeze puffed through. Then came the real rain, with lightning, thunder, and hail. Fixing drinks, I cut limes for sidiki and tonic, and for ice I scooped up some of the banked hailstones. Othman and I sat under the overhang on the terrace sipping our ozone-tanged drinks.

"Is that really a Saudi princess in there?"

"No."

A brilliant rainbow appeared as the sun penetrated a rift in the clouds. Right below us, across the street in the cinder-block factory, the two barefooted Yemeni men who worked and lived there, in one of those block houses I described earlier, chased each other over the wet mounds of sand in a game of tag, as innocent and frisky as calves or kids at day's end. At the pump the water carriers, who had stood in a doorway to escape the downpour, filled their shiny buckets and resumed their tireless shuffling trot.

"Is she a Saudi?"

"No."

The soldier who regulated traffic at the middle of the intersection, who had also sheltered in a doorway, mounted his pedestal and began moving and stopping cars, trucks, and donkey-pulled water carts in this newly dripping world by hand-turning a pole to which green and red flags were attached. It was a dangerous job. His life expectancy was about the same as a tail gunner's of a B-29 in a dogfight. A black Cadillac with a white *thobe* in it sped by, blaring a warning with the first seventeen notes of "La Cucaracha" on its musical horn.

"Does Tony know this?"

"No."

"What is she?"

"Egyptian whore."

"Shall I scoop up some more of this ice and get us another drink?"

"Hell, yes!"

The mysteries of the East. While Tony was having his revelations, I was having my own as Othman explained that the woman was a belly dancer whom an older Saudi had greatly admired in a nightclub in Cairo, and had married. Prostitution is illegal, but a Saudi with money can marry and divorce as often as he pleases, so long as he doesn't have more than four wives at a time and provided, of course, that the wife-for-a-night (or -a-week or -a-month) is foreign, and tribeless. One might think that this practice takes advantage of the Koran's lack of fine print, as it were, but the example was set by the lusty Prophet himself, and has been followed religiously by Muslims of means ever since. The most spectacular follower in our day was Abdul Aziz ibn Saud, who had hundreds of wives. That woman plying her trade with Tony in my bedroom turned tricks while her lord was absent on business. Why not? She had no job security; she never knew when she might be sent packing, and so she was capitalizing on her scarce commodity while she had the chance.

"Then Tony paid her?"

"No, I did."

"Isn't that carrying the Mr. Nice Guy bit a little far?"

"Actually, he did. I told Tony that the princess expected some kind of gift, French perfume or something, and that I'd buy it for her if he gave me the money."

"Then what's this about him going to the shop so she could have a look at him?"

"Well, you know, that's the way it is done sometimes. But that woman in the shop was only my sister."

It's amazing what the truth will do for one. Suddenly, what seemed a secretive, even a sinister, *alien* civilization became comprehensible and human. I won't say that I felt at home yet (I had only been there a few months), but I became less ready to chuck it all and take the next flight out. My possession of a higher truth didn't help me as far as Tony was concerned, though. He was convinced that he had not only cracked the world's toughest nut, but that he had gotten the sweetest part of the meat, a Noble Princess. For him and his global ambition it was downhill all the way from here. It was impossible to be with him after this without the subject invariably coming around to women, Arabia, and what did *we* know about Saudi women? We were all glad when his contract ran out and he left. Many was the time, when he was going on about his princess, standing in the middle of the room to imitate her lascivious gyrations, that I felt tempted to tell him, but I never had the heart. He wouldn't have believed me anyway.

When we reached Taif, Othman offered to put me up in his villa, but I preferred to stay with some Americans. I knew what to expect at Othman's: despite his American ways, he, too, held court in a kind of all-male *majlis*. So I asked him to drop me off at that intersection where we had sat on the balcony sipping the hailstone-chilled sidiki. Miraculously, in the destruction and construction Taif was undergoing, it was still there, more or less intact. The policeman-on-a-pedestal had been replaced by a traffic light, the water carriers and the block factory were long gone, but there was the apartment house and the balcony. Well, who cared? Drowsy, and in need of a nap (first things first), I stretched out on the sidewalk across the street under a pepper tree, its delicate pinnate leaves coated white with construction dust, and used my pliable suitcase for a pillow. I didn't think twice about doing this—gone native, you might say. In fact, as soon as my eyes were closed and my hands folded on my stomach, with the sun-warmed concrete under me, I experienced that delicious drowsiness that comes only when I am at peace. I hadn't a care in the world. Nobody paid me the slightest attention, no more than I would notice anymore such a common sight as a man stretched out asleep on the sidewalk. Moreover, I could have spent the night there in perfect safety. This was Arabia, not Chicago; there, if a man in need of a quick snooze were to lay himself down on Main Street at five in the afternoon, they'd call out the National Guard. Arabians (except in the area of sex) are much more tolerant of human needs than Americans are.

When I awoke I was surrounded by the National Guard. Well,

not actually surrounded; the guards (an elite regiment distinguished from ordinary soldiers by their light-colored khaki uniform and *ghutras* instead of caps) were strung out along the road at hundred-pace intervals, and armed with machine guns. That meant that someone royal was coming along. As for me and the other flotsam of the street, I was glad to see that the nearest cigarette-smoking guardsman took no more notice of us than the pariah dogs.

These guardsmen were recruited from the most loyal tribes, traditionally those of Nejd, the Saud family's natural power base around Riyadh, and were essentially bodyguards. While it is true that 95 percent of the Saudis are happy with the way things are, there are always that 5 percent who aren't. Besides, since the Sauds run the country as their family business, with their own members in all the key positions of power and much of the profits going to them; and since they themselves had seized power by naked force, what logical reason was there that some other ambitious family couldn't do the same? After Ibn Saud had conquered the whole country, he used to keep his country's wealth— a trunkful of gold that he considered his—under his bed, to disburse as he saw fit. There wasn't that much. Some was brought in by the pilgrims; the rest was given him by the British to buy his loyalty, and he had to give most of that away to the Beduin tribes to buy *their* loyalty. But then came oil, and when his eldest son and chosen successor, Saud, took over, he had enough revenue left over to live like a king in a fairy tale. King Saud, as his father before him, clearly thought that the money belonged to him and his brothers and his sons. He continued to bribe the fickle Beduins, but otherwise he wasn't so much the head of a government responsible to its people as the leader of a gang of pirates. Finally, however, his luxuries and excesses became so grotesque and notorious that, out of self-preservation, the royal family ousted King Saud and called upon his younger brother Faisal, of more austere personal habits, to institute reform. It was only in Faisal's reign (1964–1975) that something resembling a modern state began to emerge. It is true that now the House of Saud no longer regards the national treasury as its own private purse, true that it no longer practices the kind of no-tomorrow ostentation that was common in the days of Saud (whose name has been expunged from the family history), but the ability and the willingness of the royals to line their own pockets is well known. David Holden and Richard Johns, in *The House of Saud*, have a description of that extravagance:

> There were, in all, ten monarchical palaces built or at least started [by King Saud] in the 1950's—in the capital, in Jeddah, Mecca, and Medina, in the pleasant juniper-clad hills above Khamis Mushayt in Asir, and on the Red Sea coast. The most remarkable example can be seen in the centre of Riyadh's wealthy suburb of Nasariya. A pink-washed palace big enough for a sun king, built only twenty-five years ago yet already all but a vacant ruin. Persian carpets by the hundred covered its acres of marble floor. Crystal chandeliers by the score lit its giant halls and stairways. In its gardens, vast fountains played by night and day, imported cage birds trilled among orange trees, and jasmine and thousands of rose bushes made the desert bloom. Turkish tiling and French brocade hangings, giant Spanish lanterns and Chinese vases as big as a man, Rosenthal dinner services for five hundred or a thousand people and gold and silver plate by the ton. [There was] a surrounding complex of satellite palaces, harem quarters, a mosque for the royal family, a school for its

progeny, a hospital for its household, and a barracks for the bodyguard employed to protect it. Around all this was built a pink-washed wall, fifteen feet high and seven miles long, with a triumphal archway for an entrance.

. . . Bribery and graft took its daily toll. Wages and bills went unpaid for months while those who should have paid them pocketed the money. Expensive palace fittings were "lost" and sold back again to the royal commissariat from shops in Riyadh and Jeddah owned by the King's "advisers". Food disappeared from the palace kitchens in the same way, and as the annual kitchen bill for Saud's ten palaces was $5 million there were rich pickings to be made from such simple robbery.

Apart from his extravaganza at Nasariya he maintained nine other palaces around the country and moved frequently from one to the other with a household of several hundred people in tow. On desert safari among his bedouin tribal friends he never moved with less than fifty vehicles and he held court in a special travelling tent palace big enough for a circus ring. His personal desert sleeping trailer, run up for him at a factory in Tulsa, Oklahoma, was reputed to have cost nearly $400,000 and contained a pale green drawing room with gilt armchairs and sofa, a pale blue bathroom with gold fittings, and a royal blue bedroom with a king size velvet bed placed beneath wall to wall ceiling mirrors. A quarter of the royal income was spent importing military equipment, much of which the unschooled Saudi soldiers did not know how to use and some of which was never unpacked from its crates. A royal yacht was purchased for $2 million and sold again for a quarter of that price because nobody could be found to sail or maintain it. Most of its equipment had been pilfered by the King's own men.

Well, not everyone loves the House of Saud, but the sidewalk slouches (including me) were obviously deemed no threat to its security by its bodyguards. They were now diverting traffic farther up, to clear the road, and any Saudi who had his car parked along the royal route and wanted to use it, as one fat middle-aged man did now (his stomach pushing his *thobe* out so far that, like a maternity dress, there was a foot of clearance between the cloth and his ankles), was out of luck. This puffy character, with an awakened-from-nap pout like a spoiled child's, remonstrated with the soldier, which I was glad to see. Saudis are not cowed by authority, and they are all such selfish individualists that a totalitarian obedience could never be imposed on them (". . . if they ever learned to queue up . . ."). After getting nowhere with the soldier, he made a gesture of despair and rolled his eyes upward, as if calling on Allah to witness. Then, with his scrubbed plump feet thrust into sandals too small for them, he shuffled toward a public telephone.

A public telephone! I never believed I'd see one in Arabia, but there it was. Canada Bell had recently buried hundreds of miles of cables beneath the desert and wired the whole country. High time, too: only a couple of years ago, Othman, with a big contract hanging on a telephone call he had to make to Italy, found it easier and quicker to fly to Beirut and use the phone at the airport.

"Ahlo!" The man shouted, as if into a speaking tube. The Yemenis got up and moved close, the better to hear. A teen-age boy coming out of the supermarket, carrying a plastic bag full of chopped-up mutton, stopped and hunkered down almost right at the man's feet. When the man reached his party he, too, squatted down, the better to talk. He did not lower his voice or seem annoyed at this eavesdropping; as I said before, there is no privacy in Saudi Arabia. When the man had concluded his shouting in

Arabic (his audience having nodded and frowned sympathetically at the ups and downs of his narrative), he stood up and finished it off with the fashionable English flourish—"Okay, bye-bye"—and waited under the pepper tree with me for the king to pass.

A police car with siren screaming cleared the way. Following that, a kind of jeep with a machine gun on the back, manned by soldiers, swayed around the turn, then two or three black Cadillacs with important-looking Saudis in white rounded the corner. Next came a black limousine with tinted windows, followed by another jeep and four soldiers on motorcycles. A small crowd of children and idlers clapped their hands for whoever it was behind the dark glass, but a barefoot Beduin who was walking along in the same direction as the motorcade, balancing on his head a bundle of green alfalfa for his goat, did not break his proud, quick, almost feminine stride or even bother to look. I rejoiced at this magisterial indifference (a product of the old desert egalitarianism) and wondered at this new pomp. Twelve years ago, when Faisal was the king and I was a culture-shocked teacher living in that apartment there, he'd go by under my balcony every Friday at noon on his way to the main mosque for prayers, sitting beside his driver in a white Chevrolet, his elbow resting nonregally in the open window. Now, *that,* I was about to say, was a king, but then I remembered what an unenlightened old fanatic he really was; and while he himself did not seem greedy, he took it for granted that all those in positions of privilege were stuffing their pockets like mad.

As I stretched and dusted myself off, I reflected that *everybody* in the Magic Kingdom was stuffing his pockets according to his ability and need, even those at the bottom of the totem pole, the Yemenis and other foreign workers who were enjoying windfall wages. I had done my best to fill mine (as in one of those publicity gimmicks where you are given one minute in a supermarket to grab all you can), and if I could have done it quickly, without the pain of having to earn it in the hardest possible way (teaching English to Saudis), I would have. In fact, I owe my modest prosperity to the notorious bribe my company paid, $45 million to Adnan Khashoggi, a protégé of the minister of defense (one of the king's brothers), to get its contract. There were lots of lesser, unrecorded bribes that went to various and sundry before the big one that made the news, but the shock that reverberated around the world for a couple of weeks was but mere seismic hypocrisy. Those global howls were not of moral pain, but an even more galling smart, that of envy. Where societies are in rapid breakdown, as they are in this era in which mankind is dancing like a spastic fool at the edge of a grave of its own digging, there is no future and therefore no accountability. With nothing to believe in, with, on the contrary, the knowledge that your society is rotten and government but a clique of privileged thieves mouthing moral platitudes to keep the taxpayers in line, all men become crooked. Whether it is chiseling as petty as padding the expense account, or a major coup like Khashoggi's $45 million kickback, the justification was unarguable: since the whole system is a swindle, this money, which was not earned honestly anyway, is as much mine as thine.

Feeling the need to stretch my legs (I had been sitting around for three days, two in Dheifallah's *majlis*, half a day in Bob's Land Cruiser and the other half in Othman's Silverado), I picked up my light suitcase and shopping bag, waved on a couple of taxi drivers who slowed down and looked at me expectantly, and began walking the mile or more to the compound, where, I knew, a warm friend and a cold drink awaited me.

Changes! Arabia's oft-stated goal, of keeping intact its religious and social values while undergoing the most rapid changes of any society in history, is like trying to keep an adobe house from crumbling in the throes of an earthquake. A miracle has been wrought here on the world's worst piece of real estate. I marvel that they were able to come so far so fast. Never mind that they had all the money in the world to do it; they started, don't forget, with nothing. What good is money if all you have to work with is a population of three or four million Beduins living in goat-hair tents, a handful of mud-walled towns, the whole in a deep sleep, its lullaby the muezzins' cry, forgotten by time and the world?

Now here's Taif, on its way to becoming the "showplace of the Middle East," as Prince Fahad put it, and it couldn't have happened to a nicer little town. If, that is, they ever finish it, and let the dust settle so people can actually live there. A whole generation of Saudis has come to maturity knowing nothing but a scarred landscape, construction and demolition, everlasting rubble. In another society, more self-pitying, any number of studies would be undertaken to show the harmful effects on the population of such sudden wrenches and dislocations. The Saudis, however, are fortunately ignorant of all this.

As I walked, the structure that used to catch my eye from afar was the dark old Turkish fort, built of gloomy stone on an outcropping of rock and casting its beetling shadow over the old souk. "In the midst of the town appears a great and high building, like a prison; that is the soldier's quarters," said Doughty. Turkish soldiers were garrisoned there, and in every other town of any size in the Hejaz and Asir from Tabuk to Yemen, in the days when the blind led the blind and Turkey had an empire. When T. E. Lawrence helped the Arabians drive the Turks out of the Hejaz at the end of World War I, his best-known exploit was blowing up the tracks of the Damascus-to-Medina railroad; the twisted rails and overturned locomotives are still to be seen on the desert. It has been fashionable (since Lawrence, I suppose) to denigrate the Turk as a boorish peasant in favor of the proud, pure-blooded Arab. However, the cities of the Hejaz region— Taif, Mecca, Jidda, Medina—owe what charm they have (and that only in architecture) to the Turks.

No matter. None of it will last to tell the tale. What the Turks built, the Saudis destroy. The old barracks have been knocked down for a new civic center, and the municipal buildings, those vestiges of a remote, flyblown, improbable empire—a sideshow of a sideshow, Lawrence called his campaign in Arabia, but that could describe the Turks' presence there as well—are coming down. When Doughty finally made it to Taif after his perilous travels, it was the Turkish administrator who welcomed him, probably in one of those newly wrecked houses through whose rubble I now wend my way. Careful of scorpions. Every time one of those plastered and blue-washed adobe walls is thudded down, scorpions that had nested in the dim recessed coolness are sent looking for new homes.

Steering toward King Faisal's old office building, a tall, white, elegant, Turkish-built structure with dark brown wooden shutters that stands all alone at the far edge of Taif out on the Riyadh road, I came, almost within its shadow, upon two busloads of pilgrims who had stopped for the evening. Although this was not the month of hajj and therefore not the official pilgrim season (when a trip to Mecca is "worth" more—in a lifetime point system every Muslim has with Allah—than one not in the pre-scribed period), a pilgrim can perform the hajj whenever and as often as he wishes. If you live in Taif, you are apt to see, trickling along any month of the year before the annual exhilarating flood, pilgrims from the poor Muslim countries to the East, looking as if they'd just stepped out of the pages of *National Geographic* magazine. Welcome, a thousand times welcome! Anything that brings color and novelty into the drab, joyless kingdom is welcome.

The ancient Mercedes buses were overloaded and sagging crookedly on their springs. Each had an eye painted on the front to find the way, and fancy Arabic script saying, "Allah be my Guide." On this their final night before the descent down the escarpment to Mecca on the morrow, there was a general airing out and housecleaning of the buses, a taking-down and reorganization of the contents of those large bundles that were lashed to the roof. The bare poverty of these peasants was obvious. The dismembered, wind-cured remains of what had begun the trip as whole sheep dangled out several windows on cords. Chunks of meat and bone were thrown into blackened cooking pots and set to bubbling over gas-bottle burners. Plump, elderly women, their white faces moon-round under white kerchiefs (the black veil is worn only by Arabian women), sat on the ground rolling and smoking cigarettes. Skinny men with faces full of hair (Turkomen, I guessed), wearing trousers baggy in the legs and tight at the ankles, and shoes that would cost a dollar at the Salvation Army, strolled about at this hour of sundown, smoking cigarettes cupped in work-roughened hands. Some of them brought out bundles of new rugs—strong geometric designs and garish colors—and unrolled them to entice a passing buyer. Other men sat on the ground with a loop of rope around their waist and knees, to help them sit longer and be more comfortable. The rugs didn't interest me, but that's because I had been spoiled by rugs that these people's ancestors had made a hundred years before. As in architecture, so in rugs: the old is better than the new.

I stood there on the rough field taking it all in, reveling in it, realizing that I had indeed seen the "old" Arabia for the last time. Taif had changed more in the last two years than in the last two thousand. As recently as 1975, Mohammed could have recognized the Taif he was thrown out of when he tried to preach to the Taifi pagans; now, even I (who had lived here for three years ending in 1977) was lost, mixed-up, turned around. I must confess that at the same time that I was reveling in the world's diversity, I also deplored it. After admiring the costumes and the exotic jewelry, wondering at the language—all surface things— what is left? What was left, I thought as I walked around to the open door of one of the buses and saw taped to the dashboard a picture of Ayatollah Khomeini, was the *mind*. Clothes, jewelry— these are mere coverings and ornaments, baggage easily discarded or exchanged. As I see it, the barbarians among us (not only in the Middle East either), ignorant of history's mistakes, are dooming *all* of us to repeat them.

A couple of the local barbers—undoubtedly foreigners, for a Saudi will drive a taxi or keep a shop in the souk but will not cut hair—had brought straight-backed wooden chairs and cloth capes and were busy cutting the hajji men's hair and shaving the shorn skulls (suddenly small and fragile-seeming, like birds' eggs) with a safety razor. Some of the men shaved their heads but only trimmed their curly black beards, which gave them a look of peculiar fierceness: a Crusader would have quailed at a lonely meeting in a dark alley. This dedication ritual prepares the pilgrim for his next step, the donning of the dedication garb, two clean, white pieces of "cloth without seams." Terry cloth (made in the West, of course) is the preferred material, one towel tied around the waist like a skirt, the other thrown over the shoulder, the *left* one, because the right arm must be free for "lapidation"—

stoning the Devil—once the pilgrim reaches Mecca, and the stones must be thrown with "enough force to expose the right armpit." (After arriving in Mecca the pilgrim must follow a set of detailed, nit-picking instructions that would stun a lawyer.)

Only fifty years ago, the pilgrims furnished the sole revenue for the impoverished, newly fledged kingdom. (Standard Oil was drilling, yes, but coming up dry.) Ironically, today they have become a considerable financial burden, since some thought is now taken to protecting them and making them comfortable, rather than merely fleecing the hapless innocents. The millions of riyals spent, however, is cheap considering the amount of propaganda the royal family is able to milk from the annual affair. The pilgrims pour in by the hundreds of thousands, and Saudi television plays it for all it's worth. In the Muslim world, it's the biggest thing—the *only* thing—that happens of interest in their long bleak year. It's the equivalent of the World Series and the Democratic Convention rolled into one. A sort of national bed-lam reigns. Airports—never places of decorum anyway—are thronged with shouting, struggling people and their mountains of bulging suitcases tied with rope to hold them together. Hundreds of buses roll westward from the East, carrying thousands of pilgrims like these before me now. Also converging on Mecca from all points at this time are Beduins hauling pickup-loads of sheep that they sell at inflated prices to the pilgrims, for Islam, may Allah forgive it, is an animal-sacrificing religion. Since the Beduin, with his foot to the floorboard, drives with about as much sense of social responsibility as an escaped convict, sheep are bumped out of the shallow bed at particularly bad bumps and holes, so that you have to swerve to miss their bloated or truck-mangled bodies every few kilometers. *Khalas!* No need to stop, for if an animal is not killed in the prescribed way (its head turned to Mecca and its throat cut), its meat is not lawful. Besides, "this hollow, fainting country" (as Doughty called it) has now such a surfeit of imported meat that most of the sacrificed animals are bulldozed into trenches and covered with sand.

In the same way that the media have twisted American religious holidays and even sporting events into occasions very nearly patriotic and certainly self-perpetuating, so Saudi TV at hajj time, its announcer in his breathy references to Allah as unctious as a seducer in a radio drama, goes on a binge of self-congratulatory piety. While Mohammed mandated the pilgrimage, the Saudis certainly take credit for it all. You'd think they'd invented it. Gone are the days (not so long ago) when the pilgrim risked life and limb getting to Mecca. But what an age is ours! Now, clad in towels, pilgrims fly six hundred miles an hour above the desert thirty thousand feet below.

But what they had to endure, only fifty years ago! They would have had to wait for the Month of Pilgrimage, *Dhu Al-Hijjah*, join a school of armed pilgrims, hire guides, and hope for the best as they toiled through the dangerous sea of sand. It is a hard thing the Prophet called for: a pilgrimage to Mecca for every Muslim once in his lifetime (if he could afford it). Well, that was good business for the Meccans, and always had been. (Mohammed almost ruined it for them by his zeal for reform, and in retaliation they tried to kill him.) But of course Mohammed could not have known that his inspired word, spread by sword like wildfire after his death, would reach such bizarre, unheard-of places. When he died, his followers only numbered a few hundred misfits in the Hejaz (the area around Mecca and Medina) where he was born and died. Once Islam had spread, however, the sharks in the sand-sea, those hunger-pinched Beduins who preyed on the pilgrims, couldn't believe their luck. Pagans themselves,

I imagine it took them a long time—like the prehistoric farmers along the annually flooding Nile—to notice a repeatable pattern behind the yearly miracle. *Now* look: pilgrims wearing towels and Beduins' sons carrying briefcases leave crisscrossing vapor trails high above it all. I think that the entrenched behavior we call culture is change-resistant more from lack of opportunity than choice, like a couple stuck together in a bad marriage by the glue of poverty. Misguided cultural relativists who would preserve cultures (even the headhunters', I suppose) at all costs, don't realize that a culture is a people's way of adapting to circumstances, or of having their behavior imposed on them by a priestly or ruling class. Change those circumstances, give them something better, and you'll see how quickly, even gleefully, the members of that culture will let it perish. It *is* happening in Arabia right now. Although the picture of a prostitute-stoning religious zealot taped to the dashboard does not raise one's hopes for the future of the human race, are these people any worse a threat to humanity than our own fundamentalists would be if they had Power, Moral Right, and the Bomb? Okay, I argued with myself, so they have lost sight of the true teachings of Islam (compassion, mercy, charity), and are following, instead, one of its bloody sons of darkness, but how many *true* Christians can you name?

"Allah!" squawked the loudspeaker on the mosque nearby. The Arabian day is regulated by the muezzin's amplified wail as surely as medieval Europe was by church bells. When the men began to draw together for prayer I moved a discreet distance away. The women did not form their own prayer groups; I lost sight of them as they melted into the falling night. Probably, with more common sense, they went to seek privacy. The sky above the western escarpment still had a greenish tinge of fading light as the men faced Mecca, only an hour's drive for them now. Low and bright above Mecca was the evening star, called Ashtar by the pagan Arabs, and worshiped by them. Centuries before Mohammed they worshiped and made pilgrimages to a stone that fell out of the sky near Mecca. Mohammed gave their worship a new name, Islam (literally "submission"), and restricted it to one god, Allah, in place of the many. But the stone, and Mecca, are there yet, and the people still turn toward them in prayer as they did in the days before Mohammed.

❖

I have never been to Mecca (off limits to nonbelievers), but in my kitchen hangs a large framed color photograph of the Black Stone. This greenish-black meteorite is slightly elliptoid, or at least the visible, public part is, and only a little bigger around than a man's head. That is not so remarkable. Neither are its murky, smoky depths, or its glassy polish—rubbed, stroked, kissed as it has been over the centuries by millions of rough hands, trembling lips, and blissful tongues. What is remarkable—very remarkable—is the setting for this religious jewel. Every person who comes into my kitchen asks, "*What* the hell is *that?*"

"What does it look like?"

"It looks like . . . a big . . ."

The stone is set in a corner of a square building in Mecca called the Kaaba, a word derived from *ka'b*, the Arabic word meaning "cube." Muslims believe that it was built by Abraham (Ibrahim). Abraham was one of those proto-mythmen like Paul Bunyan, who couldn't possibly have been everywhere, and done everything, ascribed to him. One of the things he did, on a fly-buzzed afternoon among the thorn trees, was hear Yahweh's, or Allah's voice commanding him to sacrifice his son, Isaac (or Ishmael). When the knife was upraised over the boy's chest (I would guess Isaac/Ishmael never quite trusted old Pappy after that), that same voice, or one like it, ordered Abraham to kill a passing sheep instead. This is the man who is revered by three religions! Well, anyway, the Kaaba is a nearly cubic stone-and-mortar structure about fifty feet high. Over it, like a slip of lingerie, is draped a huge black cloth worked with gold thread in which the name of Allah is calligraphied ad infinitum. This dramatic black and gold (which are the colors of Beduin women's *wedding* dresses, by the way) give the Kaaba its arresting quality. Otherwise, it's about as interesting as a cinder-block, windowless warehouse.

Back to that photograph. The composition of it is so weirdly grotesque it's a wonder it was allowed to be taken, much less reproduced and sold, and to infidels, at that! The cynical ancient Greek or Roman who prayed to God to let his enemy publish a book (so that he could ridicule it), would have been filled with savage glee to have gotten hold of something even better: a closeup shot of his enemy's religious fetish. Don't get me wrong. I do not consider Islam any more a threat to mankind than Christianity or Judaism; in my view, no religion has the edge, in either absurdity or potential for mischief, over any other. But if one wanted to be hostile, this fetish is almost too good to be true as an object of ridicule.

It's all there, unmistakable: a wide band of handworked silver showing the labia, the clitoris, and the posterior genitalia tapering to the perineum. The stone itself holds open the entrance to the vaginal canal, which, fully stretched, accommodates the shiny meteorite like the dark wet crown of an emerging head; either that, or a raid-surprised lover, finding the enemy at his tent, withdrew on the run to leave the coitus-stretched tissue open for one surprised, depth-viewing moment. This naked, open-legged, shocking view into the heart of the mystery is appalling in its vulnerability. Next to it, standing in profile to the viewer, is a thin-lipped, slit-eyed, hawk-nosed Semite with an angry jut of beard, his right hand resting comfortably near the clitoris, his left hand holding the stem of a sun-fending umbrella: a patriarch keeping jealous watch over the Female. In case there is any doubt of his authority, he is wearing a khaki bush jacket over his white *thobe* and a khaki *ghutra* on his head, identifying him as a soldier of the National Guard. He is there to see that the pilgrims who come to fondle and kiss do not get carried away, harm the fetish, or trample each other getting close to it. If any other trapping were needed to complete the suggestions of coy, haremlike modesty, it is there: a black garment covers the abdomen, the mons veneris, and everything else, except for an opening, stitched 'round with white canvas, just large enough to bare the biggest, the oldest, the most famous vulva in the world.

The stone's the thing, of course, but the whole body of the Kaaba, like the total woman, has its fascination and uses. The hajjis circumambulate it seven times in a direction that, like the demented swirl of a tropical depression, is counterclockwise. Those who can get near it stand along the base with their hands up in a beseeching manner, or they actually weep, exactly like their stone-struck cousins at the Wailing Wall. Or else they sit on their bare heels and gaze ravishingly at it. Those lucky enough to get trampled to death go straight to heaven. Mohammed thought of weaning the Arabians away from their Kaaba, but instead he wound up prudently incorporating it into the new religion but changing certain of the rituals in the same way a new commanding officer might shake up a company superficially, making a few cosmetic changes just to show the troops who's in charge. Tradition. Monkey see. The Caliph Omar, in fact, who succeeded Mohammed, once addressed the Black Stone: "Had I not seen the Prophet kiss you, I would not kiss you myself." And so it goes, down to this day, pilgrims rushing to kiss an object whose shape, if they could only see it (as any outsider can) would profoundly shock them. With their lips, if not with their consciousness, they pay homage, not to Allah, the male god grafted onto paganism by Mohammed, but to something much older and much more fundamental, which the male of the species is doomed to spend his life chasing, courting, and propitiating. Religion and women!

❖

Riyadh: Dammam

Cautionary cartoons in the airport toilet. Crazy man on the plane. An Egyptian doctor. A repressed society. The Otaibis. Taxi driver. Brits flogged and an American "executed." Train station in Riyadh. Prayer obligatory. Pushy Pakistani. A queue-jumper—me. All passengers pull curtains. Crescent dunes. How Saudis pass the time. Eating *kepsa*. Rapists stoned to death in Hofuf. No man-made thing lasts thirty years. The Hotel Balhama in Dammam. The "meaning" of the Koran. A young "radical." Aramco a benign presence. Gulf flies. Taxi driver with burn scars. Nostalgia for the old days. A near miss. Blood money. Ancient civilizations under these dunes. Climatic changes. Some "long" trees.

While I had come into the Magic Kingdom a month ago at Jidda, I had made arrangements to go out at the opposite side, at Dhahran. Except for the dimming hope of running across that elusive, probably extinct, pre-Islamic woman, and a passenger train from Riyadh to Dammam I wanted to ride (the only stretch of track in the country), there was nothing else I wanted to accomplish. Instead, *that* feeling—of being trapped in the Land of the Living Dead—came over me again, just as it always had when I had lived and worked here. In a panic I looked in my passport to reassure myself that the exit visa was there, that there was no mistake—the wrong *year*, perhaps? No, there it was, and three days still remaining. Because I didn't want to risk another breakdown in a Jimps, I booked a flight to Riyadh.

Before my flight, in the clean public toilets of the airport, I faced two official cartoons, laminated plastic signs fastened to the inside of the booth's door. The first of the two cartoons had a big red disapproving X drawn through it, and it depicted Abdullah—the typical Beduin bumpkin—doing everything wrong: squatting on the rim of the toilet, the tile floor awash in paper and water. The second picture displayed a red check of approval, and it showed a *modern* Saudi sitting demurely on the john, the floor around him clean, the toilet paper on its roller, the king on his throne, and God in his heaven.

As soon as we had left the runway at Jidda, where I had gone the day before to look up a friend and visit Eve's tomb (how far back can you get?), I became aware of shouting and a scuffling commotion at the back of the plane only a few seats behind me. Since any unfamiliar noise, or even a preoccupied look on a stewardess's face, can convince me in an instant that the plane is about to go down, I pictured the worst right away: a hijacker with a bomb who would blow us out of the air. Turning, I saw two male stewards and a couple of stewardesses struggling hard with a tousle-haired Saudi in a white (but dirty) *thobe*. The two men who had been sitting in front of the thrashing man rose from their seats, wiping the backs of their necks with handkerchiefs; I heard the word *kelb* (dog) and *majnoon* (crazy), and when the stewards ceased their violent restraining and stood back, I saw that the man had been gagged, his head tied to the back of the seat with towels. He had already been straitjacketed and buckled into his seat, so that he looked pretty well pegged down, but on takeoff, apparently, he had begun foaming at the mouth and spitting. Now he rolled his black eyes wildly, like a terrified and dangerous animal. Though his mouth was stuffed with a towel, and the sounds he made were like those of someone being choked underwater, he still managed to gurgle out a strangled approximation of *Ullah, Ullah,* over and over.

Violence depresses me. Violence aboard a plane scares me. I was afraid that he would somehow get loose and do something desperate, like open the door. Since the young man next to me was dressed in Western clothes, I hazarded a remark to the effect that, while I was generally for the underdog, I hoped that, in this man's case, Allah would not heed his cries for help.

"He is not asking for help," he said in perfect English. "He was cursing God and the country. I do that too sometimes," he added, smiling.

He offered me a cigarette. Everybody on the plane was lighting up, and some were getting out of their seats to walk around, although the No Smoking and Fasten Seat Belt signs had not been turned off. Frankly, I was glad to see this: if the aisles were full, the man could not easily reach the door even if he did get loose. "They are taking him to the asylum in Taif," he added. My smoking neighbor turned out to be a doctor, an Egyptian educated in London and Canada (this all came out in a light British accent during the fifteen minutes we were aloft). He was now working in a hospital in Taif, since it was impossible for him to make a living in his own country.

"At the asylum?"

"No, thank God. Although I do have a friend who works there. He says it's unbelievable. Like Bedlam."

It is amazing how one word will open the door to a world of

shared cultural experience. Here we were, two strangers, for-eigners to each other, whose education and shared values joined us in a kind of ironic opposition to the culture in which we found ourselves.

Actually, it occurred to me that this plane could stand as a symbol of Saudi Arabia: made in America, flown by a bilingual and American-trained pilot (who introduced himself as Captain Otaibi), it was full of men who were smoking imported cigarettes, wearing imported watches and shoes and clothing and carrying imported briefcases; a plane and a society hurtling along toward the twentieth century, and hauling one of its dissidents—violently cursing God and country—to the loony bin in Taif.

I have no idea how many crazy people there are in Saudi Arabia, but my guess is that, by comparison to the United States, there are few. I mention this only because, out of all the Freudian whoppers we have swallowed whole in the West, one persistent one is the idea that "repression" brings on "sickness." Well, Arabia is a very repressed society. If children here hate their parents, they guiltily keep it to themselves and maintain every form of respect; if a bored wife has any notions about jazzing up her life through an adulterous affair, she had better think again; and a teen-age girl on fire had better cool off in some way until her father can find her a husband.

Repression! In our society we don't know the meaning of the word, yet our asylums, jails, and streets are full of lunatics, de-viates, thieves, killers, dope addicts, child-abusers, rapists, and winos. In Arabia the Repressed an unbalanced person is a sight so rare as to be shocking, whereas in permissive New York you are afraid to meet the eyes of half the people on the street for fear of encountering unrepressed madness. The doctor and I ex-plored this paradox, and another one, even more unflattering to the Western way of life. He pointed out that while we treat our insane more humanely than the Saudis, they are profoundly shocked at the way we dispose of our aging parents, by putting them away in nursing homes.

On the ground for a few minutes in Taif, I breathed a lot easier when the madman was carried off tied to a stretcher. In the air again for the hour's flight to Riyadh, the multinational stewardesses (no Saudi women, of course, are allowed to do this kind of work) busied themselves serving that "grossly contaminated" Najran bottled water, while Captain Otaibi announced in his American accent that we were flying at six hundred miles per hour at an altitude of twenty-eight thousand feet. If Captain Otaibi looked out his window, he could see the black tents of some of his Beduin brethren down there five miles below us, for we were flying now over the traditional Otaibi tribal turf, that wasteland that stretches from Taif to Riyadh. The Otaibis were—and still are—a large, formerly truculent tribe who constituted a formidable obstacle to the Sauds' efforts to gain control over all of Arabia. Powerful, and jealous of their rights, they had no wish to be ruled by their neighbors the Sauds. They resisted most bitterly, and since this warfare was only yesterday, relatively speaking, and even though the potent Abdul Aziz ibn Saud made a policy of marrying pretty girls from the conquered tribes to cement political alliances (and to indulge himself in his only real pleasure), all the old wounds are not healed. Nobody was surprised that the ringleader of the radicals who tried to take over Mecca was an Otaibi. (Had he been successful in toppling the Saud regime, instead of getting his own head cut off, the world would now be sending its ambassadors to Otaibi Arabia.)

Captain Otaibi made a perfect landing on the desert runway at Riyadh, the capital, where the temperature was 106 degrees

Fahrenheit at eleven in the morning in the month of May. Their silver wings shimmering in mirage, I saw two American AWACS parked. To help Iraq in its war with Iran, I supposed.

The taxi driver wanted to know, when he had ascertained that I was an American, if Carter was still president.

"Carter *khalas* [finished]. Reagan is president."

"Is he a Jew too?"

"No. None of the American presidents are Jews."

"If they are not Jews, why do they give Israel billions of dollars and make war on the Arabs? The Jews own America. They have all the money. Radio, TV, and newspapers belong to them. They are always making propaganda against the Arabs. I have question for you: how many states in the U.S.?"

"How many states? Fifty."

"Wrong," he said triumphantly. "Fifty-one: Israel. All the Jews in America rich."

"There are all kinds. Rich ones, poor ones. There are not many poor ones."

"They get all the money. Our prophet kicked them out of Arabia because they cheated the Muslims and got all the money. *Wallah, Yahood, mohkh katheer* [By God, the Jew is slick]. *Arab, ma fee mohkh. Keslan* [The Arab, no brains. Lazy]."

Riyadh sprawls in a haze of heat and construction dust on a flat gravel desert. As late as 1940, it was only a little mud-walled oasis town. But alas, it was the stronghold of the scowling Wahhabis, who disapproved of everything that lightened the burdens of life, such as drinking, smoking, card-playing, singing, and whistling. It was from this austere place that the Sauds and the Wahhabis made holy war on the tribes of Arabia until they had conquered them all. For the tolerant, enlightened folk (those few concentrated in the Hejaz region—Taif, Mecca, and Jidda), the Wahhabi takeover was a disaster comparable to a fundamentalist preacher and his ultraconservative followers taking over the U.S. When those internecine struggles were going on, nobody but a few Englishmen in the foreign service knew where Riyadh was, or what Saud and his bloodthirsty Ikhwan were doing. Now, big jets lumber in to land at the international airport, and foreigners like myself (fifty years ago I could have been killed like a dog by some zealot) ride around in taxis through the torn-up desert, holding edifying conversations with a native son:

"You married?"

"No. Divorced."

"Better to be married. *Zug-zug* every day." He was a comfortably fat man whose stomach almost touched the steering wheel of the Datsun. He laughed, pleasantly, man-to-man, and demonstrated the benefits of marriage by grabbing the wheel and rotating his hips.

Usually, I try to protect the Saudi from the shocking facts of American life. But I have a mischievous streak: "In America you don't have to be married: *zug-zug* anyway."

Then I told him of a young woman friend who lost count of the men she had had sexual encounters with after her hundredth. Admittedly her experience was not the norm, but it was not unique, either. Many young women of her age (twenty-three) and status (college-educated, career-minded) have had many lovers, with no end (or marriage) in sight.

"This woman is not a whore?"

"No. She sleeps with men she likes."

"Is she very ugly?" he asked shrewdly.

"Not at all."

"Does she have a father? Brothers?" (To put her to death, he meant.)

"She does. But she lives alone, works, has her own money, and does what she pleases."

"Al-lah."

This kind of independence is exactly what the Saudis fear most, for they—of all people, constantly on guard against "female weakness," as they call it—know perfectly well what their women would do if given a chance. Let her drive a car, hold a job, mingle freely in society, and *khalas*, it's all over. While it's true that young Saudi girls are now allowed to go to school, until recently they didn't learn anything except the Koran and some home-making skills. Still, all their classmates and teachers are women.

I told him about the madman on the plane, but either he didn't understand me, or the thought of an American woman taking all those lovers and going unpunished for it had rattled him. He glared fiercely and said, "Here, we take all the crazy people, the thieves, and the people who *zug-zug*, and . . . *zass!*"—he chopped at his neck with his hand more like the angry old reaper of the Old Testament than the Allah who, according to Mohammed, was merciful, forgiving. "Every Friday," he went on, "everybody—Saudis, Yemenis, Pakistanis, Sudanese."

"Americans too? English?" I asked.

"*Kulu* [everybody], same-same," he assured me with grim pleasure, his vengeful inner eye lighting up at the vision of the sword swishing down upon the pink nape of a kneeling American girl. "Last Friday, it was two Pakistanis."

"What had they done?"

"Robbed a man's house. Man came home and caught them at it, they killed him. I saw them get it. Executioner steps up: *zass! zass!* One, two! *Khalas!*"

"Did you ever see an American killed?"

"In Dammam a long time ago. You know, two Englishmen were flogged here in Riyadh recently for selling sidiki. You should have seen them, with their shirts off. They were scared as rabbits."

"Do you drink sidiki?"

"Do you know where I can get some?"

"No. What about the American?"

"You ever heard of Ibn Jaluwi?" (He was the governor of Al-Hasa, the cousin who helped Abdul Aziz ibn Saud kill the governor of Riyadh in a coup d'état, and so strict in the law that he once ordered a Beduin's toe cut off for poking at a fallen bag on the ground with his foot to see what was in it.)

"Yes."

"He was a tough man! One day an American driving a bulldozer ran over a Saudi and killed him. He refused to pay blood money. He wasn't sorry for what he did, either, and made the mistake of cursing and fighting with the police who came to put him in jail. 'You can't touch me,' he said, 'I'm an American.' Well, Ibn Jaluwi ordered him tied up and put on the ground. The brother of the man who was killed ran the bulldozer over his head. By God, it was smashed as flat as a piece of bread, as round as this steering wheel."

Although I had heard that story from my students, I didn't believe it. The Saudis, however, love to tell it, and they always emphasize that part where the arrogant foreigner thought he could treat Saudis and their laws with contempt because he was an American, and how he got the surprise of his life.

The train station was at the edge of town (in these sprawling, centerless desert cities, the "edge" can be anywhere) in an area that, in its perpetually shoddy and unfinished state, reminded me strongly of the Mexican towns that bake helplessly in the desert sun along the west Texas border. The station itself, however, was modern and air-conditioned, with joined rows of molded plastic chairs and a clean, vinyl tile floor. There was no ticket window, only a man asleep on the floor and a bored, skinny soldier with dirty shoes, half-asleep on a chair.

"This the train to Dammam?"

"*Aiwah* [Yeah]."

"Where can I buy a ticket?"

"*Badayn* [Later]."

I took a seat facing the window overlooking the platform and the tracks. There was no train, only the rails shimmering in the sun, and just beyond the fence (a catchall for windblown trash) was a tin-and-plywood shack partly shaded by a dusty salt cedar tree. A bare-chested Pakistani in a wraparound red skirt and flip-flops stepped out of it and threw a panful of water onto the sand. That done, he stooped and went back inside his hovel. The skinny soldier dozed in his yellow plastic chair. The man on the floor slept on. Outside, there was that ear-humming 106-degree heat, the broken-down fence, the shack, the pitiful tree, and a background of vague, half-completed or abandoned cinder-block structures. It was a hell; and although I knew that Riyadh was bloated with money and had many sumptuous, walled villas with Mercedes parked outside their gates, they sat, those villas, on their raw, treeless lots open to the pitiless sun—in hell.

In an hour the prayer call sounded. One is never out of earshot of a cinder-block mosque with its loudspeaker. The dozen or so men who had come in by then began gathering behind a leader, to face Mecca and begin their prostrations. The soldier joined, and the sleeping man was awakened. Up and pray! He grunted irritably and flicked his *ghutra* over his face, as if to continue his nap. But he got up after a minute, bleary-eyed and tousled; went outside to wash, and, too late to join the group, stood somewhat behind them. He went through his motions from the beginning, but out of sync, like oil-pumping rigs rising and dipping at different intervals.

When they had finished, the soldier took me outside to a barred window attached to the waiting room. The man inside selling tickets was a Pakistani. Another Pakistani stood in front of me, and a third Pakistani behind me was impatient to get ahead of me. Matching the deed to the wish, he moved around and got an elbow and a hip between me and his countryman. He was able to do this because, standoffish Anglo-Saxon that I am, I had left a fastidious two-foot space between myself and the other man. Middle Easterners have a different sense of personal space than we do. Whereas I get positively antsy when I am crowded too closely in a line, Pakistanis (and Saudis) do not feel that they are making satisfactory forward motion in a queue (assuming that it doesn't break down entirely into a free-for-all) until they are all touching, fore and aft, and breathing warmly down each other's necks.

I have heard apologists for the nonqueueing races of the world excuse them by saying that in their innocence they do not understand the queue, but that is nonsense. The queue is the embodiment of common sense. The justice of it makes immediate sense to every human being, Eskimo or Hottentot, but there are always some selfish bastards who find it inconvenient to observe the little decencies that make civilization possible. Well, I wasn't going to let this one get away with it. I was about to step forward and take matters into my own hands, when the skinny young soldier tapped the Pakistani on the shoulder and shook his head, as if to say, "Come off it, fellow, you can't get away with *that*." It is an indication, by the way, of the low esteem in which Pakistanis are held that the soldier would take the part of an infidel against a fellow Muslim. (It's interesting to note that the Pakistanis have burrowed deep into all the bureaucracies and actually do the day-to-day running of the country under Saudi bosses who are content to show up late, sign a few papers, and leave early.)

A little later, when the train showed up, I was still feeling self-righteous about the queuers and the nonqueuers. When I saw the crowd of brown and black foreign workers (nonqueuers all, I feared) converging on the gate, I grabbed my suitcase and shopping bag, determined to hold my own against the pushers and shovers of the world. As if by magic, however, I soon found myself at the gate, where I sensed that something was wrong. The melee that I had expected, that I had gritted my teeth and lowered my head in anticipation of, did not materialize. Instead, the unstable swirl of dusky Third Worlders had formed a long line that was being fed through the narrow gate by the skinny soldier. Having barged ahead to this point, with the line stretching decorously along the fence and me out there to the left of it, all alone, I stopped.

The soldier was letting the men slip through one by one—a Sudanese, two Koreans, a Pakistani—like a farmer counting his sheep, and then I saw the confusion in his eyes. What to do about me? Here was I, one of the teachers, breaking the rules I had taught. His instinct was to defer. More in sorrow than in anger, it seemed, he made a motion for me to pass, but I backed away. "Sorry," I apologized, "I didn't know. Sorry," I said to the shuffling line of dark-eyed men, and I turned back—a Good Example—to take my place at the end.

There was one first-class coach, and it was half filled with Saudis; the foreign workers paid ten riyals less and sat in second class. The coach was comfortable, clean, and, judging by the sign in the w.c.—DO NOT USE LAVATORY WHILST TRAIN IS IN THE STATION—made in England. Although the windows were tinted, and the sun not far off the zenith, the first thing the Saudi passengers did was to draw the red curtains, which let a filtered daylight in but blocked the view. *Every* curtain but mine was pulled down, so that we rolled through the desert in a kind of air-conditioned, rose-colored gloom. It was the very atmosphere they like to affect in their lavishly decorated cars, that of a cool, dim boudoir on wheels.

Imagine inhabiting a land so miserable that you can't even bear to look at it from a window. Arabians have little eye for natural beauty anyway—not that there is much of it around, mind you. The Arabian landscape is more properly a wasteland, a scenic vacuum, than a travel-poster desert—quite unlike our own Southwest with its canyons, buttes and mesas, and gorgeous colors. There was, however, one memorable sight that we passed when the sun was casting long shadows: crescent-shaped sand dunes called barchans, all with their backs turned to the prevailing *shamal* (north wind), and all of them—thousands of them, as far as the eye could see for twenty minutes as the train rolled unhurriedly through—seeming not to grow integrally from the desert, but to have been put there on the flat gravel floor intact, like giant croissants on a baking pan.

For my part, I could watch the world go by from a train window forever. I even look at Newark when I go through it on Amtrak, and if you can stand Newark you can stand anything. I also like to read on a train, but not until night falls. Had these Saudis, then, curtained out the unpleasant reality of their land so that they could read? No. I have never seen a Saudi read anything more complicated than a censored newspaper. You will see some older men, in the religious month of Ramadan, puzzling out the Koran, but that's it. While most young Saudis know how to read, they might as well be illiterate. In school they are taught the Koran. The religious ones are smugly confident that everything they need to know is in that one book, while the lazy and the stupid are merely glad that nothing else is required of them. Their society went directly from an oral tradition to television, without passing through literacy in between. Their leisure moments are spent talking or watching state-approved TV programs, but they never read.

The bathroom on our car was well supplied with paper towels and toilet paper, and was not dirtier than Amtrak gets when the employee in charge is shirking or, more likely, bickering with another unionized employee over whose job it is to clean the toilets. And there was a water fountain, probably no more "grossly contaminated" than the Najran water I had been drinking. There was a small club/dining car, and when I tried to get some tea and was told by a fatalistic Pakistani that there was no hot water, I felt I *was* on Amtrak. I knew I wasn't, however, when I asked for something to eat and a bowl of lumpy potato soup was brought me, followed by *kepsa*. Amtrak rice would have been dry and tough from being frozen and zapped with carcinogenic heat in the microwave, and the chicken would have been tasteless. My piece of chicken was a leg, half a back, and a wing, which I had to eat with my fingers, there being no utensil other than the soup spoon. This is the way I handle chicken anyway, but it greatly simplifies the operation if one is able to use all ten fingers. The Saudis, however, because of their toilet-training, use only their right hands. When I tried (out of deference to their sensibilities), it presented a spectacle about as awkward as a one-armed man trying to roll a cigarette. Happily, there were enough paper napkins, and water to wash with in the w.c.; and by the time I regained my seat it was dark, the curtains were up, and we were in Hofuf, a Shiite town only an hour from the Gulf. As Christianity has its Catholics and Protestants, Islam has Sunnis and Shiites. In Arabia the Shiites are a minority. Just as all Christian sects look alike to a Muslim, so it is hard for an outsider to see any difference between a Shiite and a Sunni. In my classes, Shiites tended to work a little harder and got better grades, but this is often the case with minorities, who have more to prove. Shiites are generally more tolerant than the puritan Wahhabis, which makes Iran's current reputation for fanaticism a great irony (Iranians are Shiites). Since the Shiites in Arabia do feel neglected by the dominant Sunnis, however, and since Khomeini sympathizers did riot in Hofuf in 1979, Riyadh keeps a wary eye on this potential Trojan horse in its midst.

It was in Hofuf that I just missed seeing a stoning. Three men were stoned, and one beheaded, for rape. Had I been there an hour earlier, I probably would have watched. I had gone to Hofuf from Al-Khobar, where I was then living, to poke around the rug souk. It was at about one in the afternoon, when the streets were empty, the shops closed, and everyone eating lunch or napping, that I came upon the three bodies. I knew instantly what I was seeing, but I think I might have needed some time to figure it out if I had not been already imaginatively prepared for it through my years here. It is, after all, one of the most shocking sights of a lifetime. By now, many people have witnessed executions. Who, in the global world of TV, isn't familiar with the gas chamber or firing squad? But television is still a film, not life, and for 3-D CinemaScopic verisimilitude there is nothing like finding yourself in a typical Saudi Arabian square (with shards of squashed Nido milk and Velveeta cheese cans, soft-drink can tabs, and thrown-out hooves and ears of butchered goats half-buried in the churned and filthy sand), in the breathless glare of a desert afternoon, seeing three bodies buried to their waists in pits, slumped like rag dolls in the abandon of death. Their hands (fingers swollen like sausages) were bound with rope behind their backs. Their crime was rape. Their mistake—I mean their strategic mistake as criminals—was that it wasn't rape *and* murder. They had not killed their victim, believing that she'd keep her mouth shut rather than live in the disgrace sure to follow if she talked. Arabian society, which will duly execute the rapist, will nevertheless always be impatient with the victim, believing that somehow—in something she did or didn't do—the woman was not careful enough. That would especially be true in this case, since she knew the men, or at least one of them (as I was to read the next day in the English-language newspaper). He was in fact a neighbor, and it was for this reason, she said, that she had accepted a ride home from the souk with him. Why didn't they kill her? Perhaps because, more than appalled by what they'd already done, they were paralyzed by fear, and so incapable of thinking through the consequences of their act. Or who knows? Perhaps they debated killing her but couldn't bring themselves to do it. Rape is one thing, but murder is something else. Whatever stayed them, letting her live meant death for themselves. She told. When the soldiers came to the house of the man who owned the car used in the abduction, they needed no further confession beyond his incoherence.

The position of the three bodies formed a rough equilateral triangle, each one about twenty yards from the other. The fourth man involved was a bachelor. Since he presumably had more incentive than the others, he was let off lightly with a decapitation. It was the three married ones that I was looking at. During the actual chucking of the stones they had worn canvas hoods. These had now been removed. The swollen, bruised faces looked calm, but it would have been difficult to recognize the features even if you had known them personally, for each was covered with a fine white dust such as a clown, or someone in the role of a mime, might use as makeup. It was as if someone, perhaps one of the relatives of the victim, had thrown a double handful of sand on each one of them when the hoods were removed. There were flies around the blood that had dried in their hair. No, they were certainly not spared the indignity of exposure.

The whole point was exposure. A man is supposed to go by and say to his son, "Well, there's Ali. And there's Saeed. And there's Mohammed over there. Come to this. With wives and children, too." How many women have been widowed in this way? I wondered. In America they would form a club, WSR (Wives of Stoned Rapists), and have monthly meetings and encounter sessions. Here, each widow (who did not choose her own husband, after all) will go back to her father, back to her tribe, whose name she never gives up. Or, if her father is dead or old, she will go to one of her brothers, and her children will be absorbed into an ongoing family, and be raised as one of them. To a Saudi, his family, his tribe, is everything. The tribe gives him his identity, his place in the world, his strength, his security, his welfare. The web of kinship is very strong and wide. Now the government is taking the place of the tribe, with mixed success. Tribe was here before the government, and it will surely be here after.

A barefoot black boy in a dirty *thobe* walked by. He was more interested in looking at me than in the bodies themselves. Perhaps he had seen it all from the beginning: the men brought by soldiers through the excited mob to the freshly dug pits. Names read out. Offense proclaimed. Punishment decreed. Last words of the condemned. The hoods placed. The crowd suddenly silent. The three piles of golf-ball-sized stones trucked in earlier for the occasion. The first stone ("Let him among you who is without sin . . .") thrown by the executioner (not the former slave; the sword is his specialty), whose job it is to act as a sort of master of ceremonies, encouraging the fainthearted, and to throw enough well-aimed stones to insure, one hopes, at least a quick unconsciousness if not a swift death. The doctor kneeling from time to time in front of each man with a stethoscope, either to signal the end, or to stand back and let the stoning recommence.

As the boy and I stood there, each of us looking at what we

found interesting, a Hofuf municipality truck puffing out blue-gray clouds of insecticide in synchronization with its one-cylinder pump—*poop poop poop poop poop*—and followed closely by a half-dozen skylarking boys, came spraying from the direction of the vegetable souk and entered the square. It sprayed the living and the dead—*poop poop poop poop poop*—and went on toward the meat souk, where carcasses hang on hooks, and where blood and offal tramped underfoot for generations on the greasy stone slabs draw millions of flies and have made vegetarians out of more than one foreigner. I held my breath as the truck passed by. The boy took off after it, laughing and shouting, and was soon enveloped in the dense, oily-smelling fog.

❖

We pulled into Dammam, on the Arabian Gulf, at nine o'clock. Dammam by night looks better than Dammam by day, which resembles a malignant tumor magnified a billion times. All of the towns of Arabia have experienced runaway growth and will, I can't help thinking, experience the reverse when the bust comes, like a film run backward. If that reversal ever takes place, it will leave the older cities, such as Taif, Abha, Jidda, Mecca, and Medina, with their original small cores. But the other cities, the new cinder-block sprawls like Dammam (which has no reason for existing except as a modern port to bring in the world's goods), will revert to a wasteland of dunes swept by hot, humid winds.

Dammam is now one of Arabia's largest cities. More exactly, it is an urban blight where a hundred or two hundred thousand people live (it's anybody's guess), half of them foreign workers. I have a hard time using the word "city" in describing an Arabian entrepôt. Arabians have little civic sense. What goes on outside his own home doesn't concern the Saudi. He'll open his villa gate in the morning and pick his way to his Mercedes through chicken bones, trash, and yellow rice thrown out there by his own household. His cities are merely uncontrolled growths of cinder-block houses, unconnected to each other by sewer or water lines, pitched on the desert like so many Beduin tents. My idea of a city is not a place where you leave your house, get in your car, and fight traffic for an hour to get to somebody else's house, where you watch TV (or, in Arabia, a smuggled-in video cassette of the latest dirty movie). A true city is a light that draws from the surrounding darkness the moths with the most sensitive antennae. It is a place where the bright and the lively rub shoulders and become civilized. It is also, however, an estuary that needs constant replenishing by tides of talented people, or else, ironically (a great city's natives are very often its worst barbarians), it gets stagnant.

Hardly any man-made thing in Arabia is more than thirty years old, or built of anything other than crumbly cinder block. I was reminded of this again last year when two of my former students, Sa'ad and Abdullah, visited me in New York for a couple of days. I took them to the tourist sights and drove them around through the various boroughs to give them some idea of the sheer size and complexity of the great city, thinking that they would be stunned. Well, they weren't. Tunnels under rivers, trains underground, high buildings were engineering marvels, true, but growing up in the Eastern province, and taking for granted Jubail, Ras Tanura, and all the fantastic growth of their own country in their lifetimes, they accepted all this as part of the modern world to which they, too, belonged. Sheer height, size, or beauty (which they had no eye for) didn't impress them. What *did* get through to them at the top of the Empire State Building—what made them look at each other with astonished surprise and ejaculate

"Al-*lah*" under their breaths—was the fact that this thousand-foot pile of stone was built in 1935, and was still standing! That's because anything in their country that is over five years old has already begun to fall apart, crumble, tumble down. Take the Hotel Balhama, which I walked to from the train station: three stories of cinder blocks studded with dripping air conditioners, set on a dark narrow street of moist packed sand and run, like everything else in Arabia, by Pakistanis. The building cannot be more than ten years old, and yet it has a rotten, crumbly look. I have heard (at first I thought it was a joke) that the native sand, wind-rounded, is unsuitable for heavy construction, and that the angular-grained sand used in certain new buildings and airports had to be imported from Sweden.

The lobby of the Balhama had probably seen some good days, when it was still new and clean and bright. Decorating the bare blue walls were four life-size color photographs of royalty, in succession: Ibn Saud, the tough-looking old patriarch with his bad eye; King Faisal the ascetic; bland King Khalid, of whom nothing bad *or* good can be said; and plump Fahad, the crown prince. (Conspicuous by his absence was Saud, whose profligate ways almost brought ruin to the kingdom. His picture is never displayed. It is as if his reign had never existed.) Generally, when I see a picture of a country's Hero or Leader in every public place, I know that the people are poor, the beggars numerous, the currency worthless, the trains late, crime rampant, and the police corrupt, but Arabia is the exception. Their Islamic state works. The only train the government has to worry about left the Riyadh station on time, real criminals are dealt with in a no-nonsense fashion, and the widespread and well-publicized briberies and payoffs are only the normal, time-honored way of doing business. The only danger to this getting-and-spending paradise are the

Wahhabist diehards, scattered but not dead. That strain of fundamentalist fanaticism still runs deep. Anathema to them are
those photographs: doesn't the Koran forbid the making of human
images? And what about those new hundred- and fifty-riyal bank-
notes, with pictures of Ibn Saud and Faisal on them: doesn't the
Koran *expressly forbid* depicting the human visage? And what
about Fahad's scandalous losses at the gaming tables at Monte
Carlo, and his drinking: doesn't Allah forbid gambling and drinking?

On the rickety table in my hotel room was a copy of *The
Meaning of the Koran,* in English, published by the Board of
Islamic Publications in Delhi, with "translation and commentary"
by one Syed Abul a'La Maududi. I turned to the sura called *Al-
Baqarah:* "They ask you about drinking and gambling. Say, 'There
is great harm in both, though there is some benefit also for people.
But the harm of the sin thereof is far greater than their benefit."
In a comment on this passage, our smug teetotaler writes, "This
was the first instruction about alcoholic and intoxicating drinks
and games of chance for stakes. At first a mere disapproval of
these things was pronounced to serve as a preliminary to their
final prohibition. The next step in this direction was that the
Muslims were prohibited from offering prayers when they were
drunk. Finally drinking, gambling, and the like were all made
absolutely unlawful." And the *like?* What, I wondered, is *like*
drinking and gambling? Feeling depressed, as I always do when
I read the Koran (or the Gideon Bible in an American hotel
room), I opened my suitcase, took out a flask of "brown," and
poured myself a shot in a water glass. Nasty stuff, but alcohol.
Thus fortified, I took up the Holy Book again: "Menses are not
only a state of impurity but also of disease. During the monthly
period, women are medically nearer a state of illness than of

health," was Maududi's learned exegesis on Allah's warning to Muslim men not to go near their wives during their menstrual periods.

I downed another slug of rotgut and turned to An-Nisa, a section containing late verses composed in Medina when the Prophet was trying to hold on to his little community of Muslims against the worldly whisperings of the hypocrites and the ridicule of the Jews. While fighting his enemies with one hand, with the other he had to ask Allah for new laws to govern his band of followers. Allah always came through with a revelation, sometimes in the very nick of time. Mohammed had to find ways of settling disputes, deciding who could lawfully marry whom, and promulgating guidelines to protect the right of orphans, especially important in light of the fact that seventy Muslims had just been killed in a humiliating defeat at a place called Uhd. Mohammed was thus a very busy man: in addition to dealing with his wives (women of his slain soldiers), he had to be, in one person, a Washington, a Paine, a Franklin, a Jefferson, and a Brigham Young.

Forbidden to you are your mothers, daughters, sisters, paternal aunts, maternal aunts, brothers' daughters, sisters' daughters, your foster mothers who have given a suckle to you, your foster sisters who have taken suckle with you, the mothers of your wives, the daughters of your wives whom you have brought up, the daughters of those wives with whom you have had conjugal relations, but not of those wives with whom you have had no conjugal relations, and it is not sinful for you to marry their daughters (after having divorced them)—and also forbidden to you are wives of your sons who are from your loins, and it is unlawful for you to keep two real sisters as wives at one and the same time, though what happened in the past is excepted, for Allah is indeed Forgiving, Merciful. And forbidden to you are the wedded wives of other people except those who have fallen in your hands (as prisoners of war:) this is the Law of Allah that has been prescribed for you.

To give some idea of the waste of time and intellect, the futile exercises that Islamic scholars still engage in (medieval angels-on-a-pin disputants would have found them congenial company; religious pedants are all alike), a footnote concerning "foster mothers who have given suckle to you" is typical. It is taken up at length, as if it mattered to us now as it did to an incestuous little tribe of Arabs around a flyblown village called Medina in faraway Arabia a long time ago:

The consensus of opinion is that the woman who suckled a boy or a girl should be treated as the real mother, and her husband as the real father with regard to this prohibition. There is, however, a difference of opinion as to the minimum quantity of milk that is suckled. According to Imam Abu Hanifah and Imam Malik, if the child suckles milk equal to that minimum quantity that breaks fast, the woman shall be treated as its real mother for marriage relations. But Imam Ahmed is of the opinion that the prohibition shall take place if the child suckles the woman at least three times and according to Imam Shafi-i at least five times. There is also a difference of opinion as to the age of the child at the time of suckling that brings prohibition. Below are given the opinions of the experts in law:

(1) Hadrat Umm-i-Salmah, Ibn-i-Abbas, Zuhri, Hasan Basari, Qatadah, Ikrimah, and Auza-i are of the opinion that if the child is suckled during the period when it has

not yet been weaned and it lives on suckling, the prohibition shall be effective; but if it is suckled after it has been weaned, it will not apply; for this is like drinking water. There is also a saying of Hadrat Ali to the same effect.

(2) Uman, Ibn-i-Mas'ud, Abu Hurairah and Ibn-i-Umar (Allah be pleased with them) are of the opinion that the prohibition will be effective if the child suckled at any time up to the age of two. Imam Shafi-i, Imam Ahmad, Imam Abu Yusuf, Imam Muhammed and Sufyan Thauri also agree to this. There is also a saying of Imam Abu Hanifah to the same effect. Imam Malik also agrees to this, but he says that the prohibition shall apply even if a month or so exceeds the time limit of two years.

(3) According to an authentic saying of Imam Abu Hanifah, the prohibition shall apply if the child is suckled during the suckling period, that is, "up the age of two years and a half."

(4) Hadrat A-ishah is of the opinion that the prohibition shall apply, if one is suckled at anytime whatsoever, irrespective of age. An authentic saying of Hadrat Ali also supports the same and Urwah-bin Zubair, Ata, Laith-bin-Sa'ad and Ibn-i-Hazam have adopted the same opinion.

I went to sleep wondering how history would have been different if the Meccans had succeeded in killing Mohammed when they had the chance.

In the hotel coffee shop, where I had breakfast (scrambled eggs, white-bread toast, and beef "bacon"), the background music on the radio was "Bojangles." I felt nearly home. Aramco broadcasts news and three music stations (popular, C and W, and classical) over a limited area. Intended originally for the American community around Dhahran, it enters as well the homes of many bilingual and Americanized Saudis. Aramco TV, with its innocuous sitcom fare, is more popular with the Saudis who live within its limited range than the local Arab stations. The coffee was American too, an insipid beverage no darker than tea. Feeling peevish anyway because of my encounter with the meaning of the Koran the previous evening, this sorry drink only heightened my pessimism regarding the perfectibility of the species. If there is any hope, then why, for example, has instant coffee triumphed all over the world? Why does a bad thing always drive out the good?

The only other person breakfasting in the small hotel dining room was a young Saudi. He was using his knife and fork on the "bacon" with a practiced hand. Catching my eye, he winked and said, "I wish this was the real thing."

"I wish this coffee was the real thing," I answered, pushing my cup aside and lighting my pipe.

"I really love good Canadian bacon. Sliced thick and fried with eggs. Yum."

"Pork is *harram*." He smiled at my use of that word.

"It was forbidden to the first Muslims."

"It still is. Why do you think that bacon you're eating is all beef?"

"In Mohammed's day pigs were dirty. They carried diseases. He was right to tell the people not to eat them. But he didn't mean that the pig was *harram* to the Muslim forever."

"Your ulema wouldn't agree."

"I don't care about them. I can read the Koran and I can think. I decide for myself about these things."

I felt like jumping up and clasping his hand like a brother, like a fellow Rationalist in Fool's Paradise, but I only said, "How do you feel about alcohol?"

"I drink like a fish," he said with a grin. "I am a Muslim, but

I do not believe our Prophet meant to punish us. People who cannot handle alcohol should not drink. That's what he had in mind."

"You seem pretty sure."

"You have to see things in their historical context."

"Right! But not many Muslims do. Do you talk this way to them?"

"With my friends who went to college, yes. With the others, I wouldn't waste my breath."

"Where did you go to college?"

"Eugene, Oregon."

"Nice town."

"I love it there. So clean. All those trees. I thought I could spend my life there, but I had to come back."

"Why?"

"Well, believe it or not I got homesick. But mostly to make money. I could never make so much money there. Maybe when I make enough money I'll go back."

"You sound like one of the foreign workers. Like my American friends. All of them are waiting until they have enough money to go home."

"What else is there to do? Everybody is bored out of his mind."

"Then why did you get homesick for such a place as this?"

"I think even if you were an Eskimo and lived in a house of ice, you would get homesick."

"I used to get homesick for Texas when I left it years ago. But I never do now."

"But you get homesick for America?"

"For some parts of it."

"And me too! Now I am homesick for Eugene."

"That's always the way. I've been homesick for Arabia . . . believe it or not," I added.

"What did you miss?"

"Oh, everything . . . the people."

"What about them?"

"I like them. They're independent and self-assured and do not try to be like somebody else. That's what's bad about them, too, though."

"How's that?"

"Because self-assurance often comes from ignorance. The more you learn, the less certain about everything you are."

"That's true. That's what happened to me. But I wouldn't want to be like I was before. No way."

"Don't you have a hard time fitting back into your old life again?"

"Very hard. It's a big problem. My father wants me to marry. A Saudi girl, naturally. But how can they send us to college in America and expect us to marry a Saudi girl when we get back? What would we talk about? Food and clothes? That's all Saudi girls know."

"Yeah, but wouldn't she get too independent if she got too educated? All of the Saudi men I know—"

"Yes," he interrupted me, "but the people who are educated are different. They know that if their wives are stupid it will pull them down—they will get stupid too. The more freedom she has, the more he will have."

"You are very unusual."

"There are many men my age who feel the same," he said and shrugged, but he looked pretty smug about himself anyway.

"What if your wife got so independent she wanted to have a lover? How would you feel about that?"

"You mean would I kill her?" He laughed.

"Well . . . isn't that done?"

"Not by the husband. It would show everybody that he cared

too much about her. He would divorce her. Forget about her. Send her back to her father. If *he* wants to kill her, that's his problem."

"What if it was your sister?"

"I might be mad enough to kill her if her husband sent her back to me and I had to take care of her. That's what I was talking about. Our women can't work and support themselves. If they could, they could go and do what they want. Like American women."

"You *are* unusual."

"Not really. We are a new generation here."

But such Western ideas *were* unusual in a Saudi, new generation or not, and he knew it, to the extent that he wore a kind of sheepish smirk, like a bright sophomore with radical views who has just shocked his elders. I suspected that the longer he was away from that college campus in Eugene, the more conservative he would become. Still, I was impressed and heartened by sentiments that are old hat on American campuses but which are truly radical in Saudi Arabia. I even got a rush of patriotic pride, which I sometimes get when I'm overseas, but never when I'm home. One of the best cures for the anti-American blahs is a trip abroad to realize that the United States has no patent on making a mess of things. America, like England, has its Irelands, blots on its escutcheon of empire, but in the case of Arabia, the American presence has been mostly benign.

Here in the Eastern province is where America got its foothold. In the 1930s some Aramco geologists, engineers, and roughnecks struck oil. In those primitive, start-up days Aramco was generously involved in seeing to the physical comfort and emotional health of its valuable employees, and so it introduced as quickly as it could the amenities of civilized life: air conditioning, a hospital, a movie theater, a radio station, paved roads, and sidiki.

A gang of Martians with their extraterrestrial artifacts could not have appeared more foreign to the natives of those dunes than the Americans. When Crown Prince Fahad remarked, during the first oil crisis, that Saudi Arabia did not want to hurt a country that had been "like a mother to us," he was speaking the literal truth. The United States did give birth to modern Arabia, and Aramco was the midwife.

The young radical and I shook hands and wished each other well. He went off into the morning to make money (he had to get a dozen Koreans through customs at the Dhahran airport, and then take them to a construction site where they would live like modern slaves in portacamps), and I went into the street to get a taxi to take me fifteen miles to Al-Khobar, my last stop.

As I said, Dammam looked a lot better (and felt a lot cooler) by night than by day. Already, at ten in the morning, the 96-degree heat and high Gulf humidity had opened all my pores. I was soaked through in a minute (in such a place, leather belts quickly get discolored by body salts). The small, pesky Arabian Gulf flies, having worn down the natives to the point where they no longer had the will to protest, could not distinguish between an unresisting local and an irritated visitor. They go straight for the mouth and eyes, and so stubbornly that a mere wave of the hand near the face only makes them grateful for the fanning. I had to brush them off; and as they are not used to being interfered with, they overlooked my rudeness and came back with new determination. Having never known persecution, all wariness and fear has been bred out of them, just like American dogs, and my exasperation at their boldness is equivalent to the shock that a Saudi visitor to the States receives when, in some mad leafy suburb, he finds himself running for his life a step ahead of somebody's unchained Doberman. We keep flies, and Arabians keep dogs, in their places.

A taxi stopped. A fifty-year-old driver with a milky film over his right eye. Trachoma, probably. When I first came to Dhahran in 1969 it seemed as if half of the older men I saw (I didn't see any women's faces) had trachoma damage. It was endemic in the fly-infested Eastern province, but now, due to the efforts of Aramco doctors and research, it has been controlled. The driver also had a burn scar on his left wrist. Many of my students from Beduin tribes bore scars from this kind of campfire acupuncture, the theory being that if you got a nail red in the fire and then sizzled yourself with it in the right place (leg, arm, neck, wrist), you would cure dysentery, possession by a jinn, migraine headaches, what have you.

"What was that for?" I asked, pointing to the scar.

"Hepatitis."

"Did it work?"

"Yeah. I tried medicine first, but it didn't help. By God, the old ways are the best sometimes."

Hepatitis, of course, either cures itself (the damaged liver regenerates on its own), or you die. Having been laid low with hepatitis here, I knew something about it. There is no medicine except rest. Saudis, however, do not believe in holistic or natural cures. They want *medicine*. I have known even educated Saudis swear that self-mutilation by branding "worked," but it is a folk belief on a level with Dheifallah's prescription of gasoline for a scorpion sting. Fortunately, Americanization (read improved hygiene) has made branding by hot nails more and more unnecessary as fewer hepatitis carriers defecate in the open, and thanks to wholesale spraying, there are fewer flies to carry the virus over the villa wall to that grape on the table you are about to eat.

"What are you?"

"American."

"*Araby helew* [Your Arabic is sweet]." By that he probably meant that I spoke it with a kind of naïve enthusiasm. My pronunciation is good, however, and what I do know comes out sounding authentic. "Did you learn it here?"

"Yes."

"How long have you been in Arabia?"

"Off and on for fourteen years."

"You have seen a lot!"

"Yes, I have. Fourteen years ago—or even five—there was nothing between Dammam and Khobar but a two-lane road. Now look."

"I don't believe it myself, and I was born around here."

In a shop window I noticed a big sign that said (in English) MERCHANDISE SALE and under it the same announcement in Tagalog (Filipino) and Thai. There were Oriental-looking men all over the steamy, sunstruck, littered streets. "Lots of foreigners," I observed.

"At one time," he said, "there were only Americans and Saudis here. There are not many Americans now. These new people are *kaffirs* [heathens]." He sighed like a man who didn't understand the world anymore. "American and Saudi," he said nostalgically, holding his two index fingers together and rubbing them slightly back and forth, "*sawa-sawa* [the same]."

❖

We almost didn't make it to Al-Khobar. That two-lane deathtrap between the two towns (now so extended that they are almost joined) had been widened and divided by a median, but that only encouraged drivers to go faster and take more chances. The wrecks littered the slopes on both sides of the sand-streaked blacktop. Many of the light poles on the divider had been hit, clear warnings of what to expect. Sure enough, all of a sudden a car overtaking us was itself overtaken by an empty Mercedes dump truck, so that, with three vehicles in the space for two, our right wheels, at 60 mph, were forced off onto the sand. We slalomed recklessly and fishtailed to a stop an inch from a wrecked Peugeot station wagon.

I was so upset—imagine, having survived so many near misses in this wild arena, only to come so close at the end—that I couldn't get a suitable curse out of my mouth while it was hot, and a cold curse is no good.

"*Allah kareem* [God is merciful]," said the driver.

If we had been injured, trapped inside a smashed car, we would have sat there until the police came. No Samaritan would stop. It isn't that Arabians are lacking in compassion; it is because they have "blood money" to worry about. If the person they tried to help died, they could be blamed for the death, and wind up in jail until they paid blood money to the dead man's tribe.

Once I saw a camel that had been struck by a car take all of a hot day to die in a ditch, although there were idlers and gawkers and soldiers with guns coming and going. I asked one of the onlookers why a soldier didn't shoot her: her legs were broken and her thirst-blackened, bloody tongue protruded pitifully. He said that if a soldier shot her he would have to compensate the owner! Foreign workers are warned by their companies not to stop and help accident victims. If a driver involved in a fatal accident lives and his passengers die, he is obligated to pay blood money. The amounts vary, but he can count on $10,000 to $15,000 per corpse. Foreigners take out liability insurance that theoretically covers them, but most Saudis don't bother. Insurance, as a hedge against the unknowable future, is an alien concept. (So, for that matter, is weather forecasting. They report the weather that was, not the weather that will be—although nothing here is easier to predict—but who can know about the future but Allah?) A man will be kept in jail after a fatal accident for as long as it takes him or his tribe to get the money together. When it is paid, he is freed. Incidentally, as a curious illustration of the Saudi's fatalistic logic, if you are the sole passenger in a taxi that is involved in someone's death, you, not the driver, are liable for the blood money. In other words, if our near miss had been a hit and someone had died, I'd have to forget about catching that midnight flight out of Dhahran the day after tomorrow. It would have been my fault. Why? Well, look at it this way: if the driver had not been taking me to a certain place, he would not have been in that spot at that moment the accident occurred, would he?

We resumed our drive. Near Al-Khobar I could see, off to the right across the sand, a bare sandstone hill (Dammam Dome) that excited the first geologists who saw it because the structure indicated the presence of oil. They began drilling, and their dusty little camp at the base of the dome became in time Dhahran, which could easily be mistaken for any Sunbelt suburb. Al-Khobar at that time (only fifty years ago!) was a nearby fishing village of a few mud-and-palm-frond shacks and would still be that today if the world hadn't needed—for war and commerce—the oil under its barren sands. Although Al-Khobar had grown beyond recognition, I judged it was right about here where I would come with my wife on a Friday (my one day off) to kick through the dunes for potsherds. Four thousand years ago, an important civilization called Dilmun flourished on the island of Bahrain, twenty miles offshore. The miserable coastline that the Aramco geologists encountered, with its pesthole villages full of flies, was once part of that civilization. The well-wrought potsherds that my wife and I picked up out of the sand came from the tumuli of buried noblemen.

On Bahrain and in Arabia near the coast there were thousands of these grave-mounds, but a few broken shards were all that was left. Robbers had long since taken anything of value. Dilmun was excavated and reconstructed by a team of Danish archeologists in the 1950s and 1960s, while other sites on the Arabian peninsula yielded cities as old as 7000 B.C. Thaj, an hour's drive northwest of Dhahran, with thick stone walls, was a city built on a lake. Geoffrey Bibby, who described the archeologists' adventures in Bahrain and Arabia in *Looking for Dilmun*, writes:

. . . I had seen air-photographs, and knew what to expect. But I was not prepared for the scale. Below lay a considerable city. . . . And around it stretched fields of tumuli. . . . We flew back and forth over the site half a dozen times while I took in the scene. . . . Everything was covered in sand and rubble, but the general outline was clear. And one thing was completely obvious.

Thaj was a city on the edge of a lake. It stretched for almost a mile along the lake-shore, and half a mile or more inland. Only there was no lake . . . to the northern side of the city stretched a large salt-pan, a *sabkha*.

Now, *sabkhas* are areas of salt mud which clearly once have been water. They are dried-up lakes. They are useless to man. There would be no reason to build a city beside a *sabkha*. Therefore this one-time lake had still been a lake when Thaj was built. This was going to tie up with our speculations on the prehistoric climate of Arabia, for only a higher rainfall, or at least a higher water-table, could have held water in the lake-bed.

There was also the legendary Gerrha, a rich city mentioned by Strabo (the first-century Greek historian and geographer), but its irrigated fields and fine houses are *still* lost under the encroaching sand. In Ubaid, on the coast north of Dhahran, painted pottery seven thousand years old has been found. Arabia is a riverless land, but its many dry wadis and gorges show that water once rushed there. Perhaps the legend is true, and it *was* the Garden of Eden. Bibby writes:

. . . Some millions of years ago in the Late Miocene, during the last great mountain-building period of the world, the Persian massif had lunged southward, tipping the whole slab of Arabia. In the east Arabia had been pressed down below sea level, forming the Arabian Gulf. And in the west the slab had been cracked off from Africa, forming the deep chasm of the Red Sea, the Rift Valley of East Africa, and the crack which was now the Gulf of Aqaba and the Jordan valley. It was not unlikely that a recovery had been going on ever since, that Arabia was gradually returning to the horizontal.

It would explain many things in the historical record. Such a rise of east Arabia would reduce the flow of underground water from the high land to the west, would in extreme cases, as perhaps here at "Gerrha" [Bibby was investigating some ruins that he thought could be the lost city], cut off the flow altogether. The exposed sea bottom would dry out and blow away as sand and dust, which would choke the vegetation on the land, already threatened by the diminishing water supply. Dust-bowl conditions would result, adding more sand to the dunes. The supply of pasture for grazing animals would diminish, and what there was would be overgrazed, giving more denuded areas, and more sand. Perhaps the whole of the sand of Arabia could not be accounted for by this one single cause, but everything would contribute to the same end. And the process had been culminating during the time when man was trying to establish his civilizations along the coast. Dilmun and Gerrha had been fighting a losing battle.

Civilization on top of civilization lay buried under these dunes, and each had its gods. Allah is now top dog in the pantheon and his name is cried from every minaret, but what about the great Inzak, who was the deity of Dilmun? Were men put to death for not believing in him? Other gods and other kings, too. One of them, the king of Lagesh, in southern Babylonia, claimed (in a cuneiform inscription from 2520 B.C.) that "the ships of Dilmun, from the foreign lands, brought me wood as a tribute." Wood! While digging for the past has not been going on for very long in Saudi Arabia, the evidence was clear: civilizations rose here and there on this coast, only to give way at last to the barbarians and Beduins, who "lived in the patched-up ruins of their predecessors," says Bibby, "scavenging the ruins for building stones, and filling the resultant holes with rubbish." Clay tablets excavated from the ancient counting houses in these trading empires show careful accounts kept of the oil, copper, millet, and wood that were bought, sold, consumed, or transshipped. It was freewheeling capitalism, getting and spending. Wars were fought for plunder or to protect trade routes, and here in front of my nose I was witnessing the latest such phenomenon on this ancient shore that has seen so many ups and downs, so many peoples come and go—built, this time around, on an underground lake of oil.

We waited at a red light. Every other vehicle was a gear-grinding, smoke-spewing truck hauling in the goods of the world:

pipes, cars, wire, cement, tractors, frozen food. I kept thinking: this is *insane*. What is going to become of all this when some substitute is found for oil?

The last truck to get through the intersection on the light was a Mercedes pulling a long-bed trailer stacked with creosoted telephone poles.

"My God, look at those," said the driver. "Where do you think they came from?"

"They could have come from Europe, but they're probably from America."

"There are trees that long in America?" (They use no separate word for "tall.")

"Those are not long trees. Those are only average trees."

"Do you have many of them like that?"

"Millions and millions of them like that."

"Al-*lah*."

E P I L O G U E

———————————— ❖ ————————————

*M*y travels were over. By and large I was content with what I'd managed to see and do, although I must confess that if I'd been shot at, or at least had my life threatened by some wicked fanatic, I'd have felt more heroic. I didn't even get sick! The Najran water I'd been drinking brought me not the slightest discomfort. It's *hard* to be a Heroic Traveler in this age of jet travel and bottled water, even if—by American standards—it *was* "grossly contaminated." Doughty, poor devil, had to drink the foulest water imaginable and was often ill, but Thesiger, with more robust plumbing, boasted of having drunk with impunity "out of every ditch" in the Middle East.

My failure to meet the Hospitable Widow, while it was a disappointment, doesn't necessarily mean that she doesn't exist off in some lost pocket of the Asir, no more than you can conclude that there are no intelligent people in, say, Tulsa just because you didn't happen to run across any when you were there. Any conscientious traveler will blame himself, when the trip is over, for not having done this and that, and I am no exception. Now that it is too late, I ask myself why I didn't follow those two wild men I saw in the Khamis Mushayt souk back to their village, where I suspect that some pre-Islamic customs may still prevail; but at the time, of course, I had a hundred reasons for not doing so.

I did, however, hear a sort of corroboration of this legend from an Englishman I talked to on my next to last day in Saudi Arabia. That day a party of us—Saudis and Americans—had gone out to the desert for a "goat-grab," which is a popular recreation on Friday, the Muslim sabbath. The point of a goat-grab is to spread rugs on the sand, drink sidiki, and smoke the *shisha* for a couple of hours in the "thin, sprinkled" shade of a thorn tree while waiting for the sheep and rice. (The meal was provided by two of our ex-students, now businessmen, who hosted the affair.) The sheep is boiled whole with spices and herbs in a huge copper pot that is tinned and shiny on the inside and crusted and blackened on the outside. When the sheep is done, the rice is cooked in the savory liquid, and when it is ready it is heaped onto a large shallow copper tray, the sheep dismembered and put on top. Then this steaming, delicious mess, carried by two men, is placed on the ground in the midst of the company.

Next to me at trayside was a woman we called (behind her back) Florence of Arabia, and her prepubescent daughter. When Florence first arrived in the country she made herself tiresome by her golly-gee espousal of every feature of Arabian life that we found distasteful or ridiculous, as if she were determined to be merely contrary, but a while later she shocked, angered, and disgusted everyone by making good on her threats to go native. She converted to Islam, and began an affair with the Saudi hostler at the stables where company wives (who could never afford to belong to the horsey set in the States) could ride around the desert dunes and pretend to be something they clearly weren't. Florence's identity crisis was greater than most: she simply could not figure out who she wanted to be. She'd try on roles for size, as she would dresses in a shop. For instance, she came back from a vacation in England speaking like the Queen (so chameleonlike was even that intimate apparel of her soul, language), and when that upper-class British mood wore off, she'd say that the Simple Life (as lived by the Arabian woman) was the best. A product of Boston's Irish-American lower middle class, her father a blustering but harmless drunk long since emasculated by her strong-willed Catholic mother, she longed for *anything different*, and in Arabia she found it. But above all, she found certitude.

While she was going through all these changes, however, she made her poor American husband's life miserable. As a new Muslim, for example, she didn't want sidiki in the house anymore. Instead of divorcing her for that, as he ought to have done, he acquiesced to keep the peace, and she repaid him by despising him. Ironically, while a million battered Third World wives would have given anything to have a kindly, gentle American like Ron for a husband, Florence was fairly hopping with indignation at the faults she was discovering in him. The more he did to please her, the less she could bear him, and the brighter and higher

rose her Saudi lover's star. While she was busy extolling the
verities of a traditional, conservative society, her husband was
doing the wash and folding the clothes and making the school
lunches for their daughter, but the thanks he got for his un-
chauvinistic disregard of traditional sex roles was ridicule and
contempt—the former behind his back from other company wives,
the latter to his face from his wife. This is all pretty standard
behavior in the course of adultery, but what made it unbearably
ironic was Florence's inability to see that the culture she found
suddenly so attractive would have put her to death for what she
was doing. To herself and to her woman cronies she kept complaining that Ron was a weak man whom she could not respect,
and if "weak" meant that he was kind and considerate, she was
right. Saudi men, she maintained, "knew where they stood," and
in that masculine assurance, she believed that their women felt
secure and were happier than Western women who, having succeeded in demoralizing their men, had so much freedom that
they didn't know what to do with themselves. Well, she had a
point, and was talking from experience, but she had a fanatic's
irritating way of trying to build a whole system on a small truth.

The irony of it all, of course, was not lost on us: as an American
woman, she had the kinds of freedoms women from other countries only dream of. Never in history have women been so carefree
and autonomous as in capitalistic, affluent America. But the
appearance, as usual, was different from the reality. Florence
could not escape an abiding sense of frustration and insecurity
that came from the fact that she was not pretty, not pretty in a
country where half of the GNP is squandered on advertising
cosmetics. To be an attractive woman in America is to have
every door standing open: to be plain is to be nowhere in the
mad mating scramble. The handsome men—the ones *she* wanted—
were pursuing the pretty women, and where did that leave her?

Free, indeed, but free to do what? To sit home alone most eve-
nings watching TV. It was this memory of being alone, and
unwanted, that caused her to defend even the Muslim's polygamy.
Since men and women are natural enemies anyway, she argued
(like her mother and father, who enjoyed each other only in
periods of physical need without the desire to be together at other
times), any woman in her right mind would welcome a second
wife who would not be a rival but a companion.

Well, these are the kinds of ideas that make for good conversation over drinks before dinner, but Florence acted on them.
The next thing we knew she had divorced Ron, married Khalid,
and had taken to wearing the *abbayuh* (black sack) and veil,
although, with her towheaded daughter trailing after her, she
looked like no other Saudi woman. We saw her often, for she
continued to get her mail in the box she still shared with Ron,
and eat the American junk food she liked in the snack bar. (The
company didn't have the heart to cut her off, although now that
she was no longer an employee's dependent, it could have.) When
she unveiled in the security of the compound, she'd have in those
first weeks an absurd smirk on her face, half proud and defiant,
half fearful, like a little girl who'd done something for which she
was afraid she'd get in trouble. Her daughter was taken out of
the American school, because now that she was a Muslim she
had to receive an Islamic education. As a female, the girl would
learn a few homemaking skills and memorize verses from the
Koran until, like a parrot, she could chant the sound but not
the sense of it. Florence even defended *this* atrocity, claiming
(again, with some justification) that American schools are little
more than hotbeds of precocious sex and drugs where an irre-
sponsible capitalism forces children into premature adult behavior
and consumerism. Poor Florence. She should have joined the

Peace Corps, or gone to college, or sowed her rebellious wild oats in some constructive way other than marrying young and then rebelling against her husband and her culture at the same time. That would have been all right if only she had not turned to a man and a society no better.

The second marriage was ill-fated. After Khalid divorced her, Florence stayed on in Al-Khobar in the apartment in which he had installed her. The *qadi* (judge) awarded Khalid the child of their wedlock (a girl), which was customary, but he made sure that this American woman, this convert to Islam with no tribe to fall back on, had a roof over her head. Otherwise, Florence got by (and kept busy) partly by tutoring English to Saudi merchants' daughters, partly by exercising horses at a prince's stable, but mostly by a monthly anonymous stipend—the gift, probably, of a philanthropic prince. Now independent and part of the Al-Khobar scene, Florence of Arabia (her "tribe" the community of expatriate Americans) became a sort of poor relation. Nobody liked her very much, but nobody knew how to get rid of her, either.

Also at the picnic was Alan, a yellow-haired Englishman who found the desert so fascinating (many Englishmen do—anything to escape Albion's chill and damp) that he spent most of his spare time four-wheeling around on it in his Land-Rover. Now, since an expatriate community has little to talk about except the host country, and since it is impossible to be in Arabia without the conversation lighting on religion and women (like a butterfly in a garden with only two flowers in it), we discussed Asir, the Legend, and the status of women in the Age of Ignorance. This didn't mean much to Alan, the kind of fellow who cared nothing about Arabia's past and took the present as he found it. (It has not escaped my envious notice, by the way, that men with this kind of phlegmatic temperament sometimes blunder into the most extraordinary adventures. Naturally, to round out his happy innocence, Alan didn't speak a word of Arabic.)

One day Alan was "bashing around" on the desert between Hofuf and Riyadh when, in the shadow of a dune, he came upon a goat-hair tent. Standing barefoot in front of it, waving for him to stop, was an old Beduin with a white beard. Alan stopped. Actually, he did know some Arabic, four words, two of which were *salaam alaykum*. When he had said them, he felt his social obligation was at an end, freeing him to shrug, grin, use sign language, and understand or not, as he chose and as circumstances warranted. In this case, the old fellow only wanted water, so Alan—a generous soul who always carried a compass and plenty of extra gasoline and water—left a five-gallon jerry can with him. While he was "talking" to the Beduin, he noticed, over a curtain that divided the "house of hair," a teen-age girl who was unveiled and who looked at him with curiosity. (Let me add that Alan was a handsome fellow.) He did wonder about the unlikely pair— an old man and a girl—some, but not much. By this time he had seen enough of these Beduin encampments (rapidly disappearing in modern Saudi Arabia) to be used to the stark, naked poverty: the black windbreak, the handful of blackened cooking utensils, a few goats inside a fold made of thorn-tree branches. The old man pressed him to have tea, but Alan cheerfully declined; the sun was getting low and he had a long drive ahead of him.

Three weeks later he was back in the same area when he ran across the same tent, same old man, same girl. Thinking to retrieve his jerry can, he stopped. He was recognized and welcomed warmly. This time he did take tea with the old man (and the girl, who drank hers standing up behind the curtain), although it was all he could do to bear the close, sun-heated stench of animals and their manure. In fact, Alan thought it likely that too many years of living like that had touched the understandings of the man and the girl, whoever she was—his granddaughter? At any rate, Alan was about to say *ma salaama* (good-bye, the rest of his Arabic vocabulary) and get back to the open, clean desert, when the man began making a peculiar gesture—hooking his index fingers together and pulling them. Not only that, he several times cast his eyes significantly in the direction of the girl, whose face had by this time disappeared behind the curtain. When these looks and gestures seemed to get no response from Alan (actually Alan was horrified that they might mean what he *thought* they meant), the old man stood up, reached for Alan's hand, walked him around to the back of the tent where the girl stood (as if she were waiting), and left him with her. The whole place, Alan reported, reeked of animals and unwashed humans. He was dimly aware that something untoward was about to happen, when it did: the girl, her eyes ringed black with kohl like a raccoon, grabbed her long purple dress below the knee and lifted it right up to her armpits. She was not wearing anything underneath, Alan said, and the sudden airing of her underskirt area did nothing to alleviate the offensive smell in the close space.

"Was she pretty?"

"I didn't take a close look, but the impression I got was that she was all there, you know."

"Why didn't you . . . uh . . ."

"I couldn't deal with it. It stank in there. It was dirty. Completely unexpected. You know, there's such a taboo on Arabian women that you come to almost fear them, and then to have one of them suddenly do something like that . . ."

"So you left?"

"Stumbled over myself getting out. They both looked disappointed, I must say. Can't tell what they expected of me. Stud service, I suppose. Shan't go back *there* anymore. Left my jerry can with them, too."

❖

We were sinfully overprovided with food. For eight people, plus a child, there were two whole young sheep and all that rice. There we were, after we had all eaten our fill, with half of it left. This is typical of Arab extravagance: it is better to throw food away rather than be perceived as too frugal. What to do with it? While eating we had noticed two Beduin women a couple of hundred yards away, grazing a flock of sheep on the scanty vegetation, threading and refining between their fingers wool upon a distaff, which they turned with the other hand. They wore the Moroccan veil, which covers the face from the bridge of the nose down.

I suggested they be invited to partake of the leavings of the goat-grab. It seemed a good idea, although the Saudis with us said they would not come over. Nevertheless we agreed it was worth a try, and so one of the Saudis got up and began walking toward the women. As soon as he had taken a few steps in their direction they yelled shrilly at him and made motions for him to stay away. He stopped, shouted something, and began walking toward them again. Abandoning their sheep, they began running away across the desert, looking back, like two defenseless creatures being stalked by a carnivore. When our friend stopped his advance, they stopped their retreat, always keeping a safe hundred yards from him. They reminded me of wild animals, or a pair of very shy cats. Finally, seeing the women getting farther and farther from their sheep, Florence called the Saudi back and, taking her daughter, began walking toward the Beduins. She spoke a little Arabic, but her daughter knew more. The women stood still and watched this strange woman (dressed, Saudi-style, all in black) with her towheaded, blue-eyed child. They even advanced to meet them over the last fifty yards, and soon we saw them all together, talking.

They stayed a quarter of an hour. When they got back, Florence announced that the women were a mother and her teenage daughter, that they had been very friendly, delighted in fact, the mother unable to resist kissing Florence's daughter several times, marveling at her fair skin, white hair, and light eyes. Would they eat? Yes, but they wouldn't come any closer than they were. Accordingly, I made up a platter of rice and meat, and accompanied by Florence, I carried it toward the women. They retreated again at this resolute advance of a male, even one bearing a gift. I stopped, they stopped. In an elaborate charade I held the tray aloft for them to see, put it on the ground, pointed at it, then Florence and I turned our backs and began walking back to our group.

"When are you leaving?" Florence asked.

"Tomorrow at midnight."

"You weren't looking in the right place," she said.

"What?"

"You didn't find your widow."

"Oh. No, I didn't."

"You weren't looking in the right place."

"Maybe not." I was about to ask where she thought I should have looked, when I met her eyes and saw the loneliness there.

"Jennifer goes to school tomorrow," she said.

When we were seated, the Beduin women walked warily toward the food, like animals sensing a trap. Keeping one eye on us and one on the tray, they closed in on that food like cats off the street who haven't learned to trust people yet. If one of us had stood up suddenly and made a move toward them, I have no doubt they would have bolted. However, they picked up the tray, went quickly back among their sheep, sat down, and began to eat. What they didn't eat they obviously saved in a plastic bag I had brought along with the food, for they brought the tray back empty to the spot where they had picked it up. Since Beduin women are not kept in a shuttered room, but must work in the open, they leave their eyes uncovered. Beduin women, it is said, are a lot freer than town women.

❖

In the departure lounge at Dhahran airport. I'm as good as out. I've got my boarding pass, I've been through passport control, my suitcase has been X-rayed, and my exit visa has been stamped with a date. I can't get back into the Magic Kingdom now, no matter what. Neither, I feel, can the Magic Kingdom get at me. It's a great feeling.

For the occasion (and for fear that the high-flying 747 would be overchilled) I was wearing a sports jacket, and in the pocket was a nip of sidiki in a makeshift flask—an empty spice bottle. The Pan Am plane on the tarmac, bathed in light and surrounded by trucks and attendants grooming it for its fourteen-hour flight to New York, was full of good booze, but I had some anxious minutes to kill in the meantime (I hate flying), and time always dies easier when it is wet. On the plane I'd sip good bourbon, but here in a booth in the men's rest room—although in this lounge I was technically out of the country, I didn't want to take any foolish chances—I downed a slug of "brown."

A month ago at Kennedy, with Arabia as their destination, the crowd in the departure lounge was noticeably glummer than this group. Then, there was an unhappy tension in the air to which babies responded by crying—and crying more loudly when their mothers tried to shush them. Men strolled about restlessly, or rattled their newspapers irritably, or talked in low, dispirited tones. But here there was an almost festive air as knee-dandled babies cooed, mothers chatted to each other behind their veils, older children, dressed in new Western clothes, played a decorous game of tag (it is rare to see an obstreperous or bratty Saudi child), and the men, dressed in business suits, talked together in civil tones. The only discordant note in this happy buzz came from an American, a guy with a big loose jaw that hung halfway open, as if unhinged. He wore a T-shirt that his beer belly pushed out like a baby bird's abdomen, and it read, in front, ARABIA— LOVE IT OR LEAVE IT, and on the back was printed a Saudia Airlines timetable. He had a friend from the same low stratum of white trash from which he himself had come. As they sat down near me I heard a churlish reference to the "ragheads and nose-pickers." It is not enough, I decided, merely to be God's spy; sometimes you must be his lieutenant, too. I got up and moved into the seat next to the prognathous lout.

"If I hear you say one more thing about the Saudis that is loud enough for them to hear, I'm going to tell that soldier over there that you have been drinking, taking dope, cursing Allah, and insulting the country. You'll never get out of here. I have Saudi friends I can telephone right now, and they can have you arrested."

I got up and moved away, but not far, only into a seat facing them, where I sat and glowered at them. Their minds were set on boil by my words, and as they sat silently simmering and watching me, you could see the lumps in their emotional stew roiling to the surface and falling, a slumgullion mixture of suspicion and low-browed rage, followed by hate, revenge, murder, and fear. Fear got the upper hand, as it usually does, and mouthing face-saving curses under their breaths, they got up and moved to a far corner of the lounge, with nobody near them. That was fine. That was where they belonged.

My nerves ajangle from this encounter, and mumbling now under *my* breath ("imagine . . . damned rednecks . . . bad-mouthing people twice as civilized as they are . . ."), I went back into the men's room and—in case they decided on retaliation and called the soldier on *me*—downed the rest of my rotgut and dropped the bottle into a trash receptacle. The sidiki calmed me. When the flight was announced I stood up, boarding pass in one hand, shopping bag containing my two notebooks full of scribbled words in the other.

When the sun rose on us we were in New York, and it was a fine June morning. The two rednecks had drunk themselves into such a stupor they were unable to get off the plane. I didn't hang around to see how they were disposed of. On the train to Manhattan, nearly every passenger had a magazine, newspaper, or book, and was reading. I was one of the few who wasn't. I couldn't take my eyes off the young women in their summer dresses.

Dale Walker lived in Saudi Arabia during its boom years, teaching English as a foreign language. This is his first published work.